Ghosthunting Virginia

AMERICA'S
HAUNTED ROAD TRIP

Titles in the *America's Haunted Road Trip* Series:

Ghosthunting Florida
Ghosthunting Kentucky
Ghosthunting Illinois
Ghosthunting Maryland
Ghosthunting New Jersey
Ghosthunting New York City
Ghosthunting North Carolina
Ghosthunting Ohio
Ghosthunting Ohio: On the Road Again
Ghosthunting Pennsylvania
Ghosthunting Southern New England
Ghosthunting Texas

Cincinnati Haunted Handbook
Haunted Hoosier Trails
More Haunted Hoosier Trails
Nashville Haunted Handbook
Spooked in Seattle

GHOSTHUNTING
VIRGINIA

MICHAEL J. VARHOLA

CLERISY PRESS

Ghosthunting Virginia

Published by Clerisy Press
Distributed by Publishers Group West
Printed in the United States of America
First edition, second printing 2011

Library of Congress Cataloging-in-Publication Data

  Varhola, Michael J., 1966–
    Ghosthunting Virginia / by Michael J. Varhola. – 1st ed.
      p. cm.
    ISBN-13: 978-1-57860-327-5
    ISBN-10: 1-57860-327-7
    1. Ghosts–Virginia. 2. Haunted places–Virginia. I. Title.

  BF1472.U6V37 2008
  133.109755–dc22

                              2008034998

Editor: John Kachuba
Cover design: Scott McGrew
Cover and interior photos provided by Michael J. Varhola

Clerisy Press
P.O. Box 8874
Cincinnati, OH 45208-0874
www.clerisypress.com

TABLE OF CONTENTS

Welcome to America's Haunted Road Trip   xi

Introduction   1

NORTHERN   7

CHAPTER 1   Arlington National Cemetery (Arlington)   8

Many locations at this burial ground for America's military personnel are said to be haunted by the spirits of those who have fallen over the past two centuries in the service of their nation.

CHAPTER 2   Bunny Man Bridge (Fairfax Station)   15

This site is reputed to be linked to a serial killer, whose spirit is said to make itself known if Bunny Man is uttered three times. Bunny Man Bridge has also influenced scenes in at least one movie and one video game.

CHAPTER 3   Gadsby's Tavern (Alexandria)   23

A beautiful young woman who died at this historic tavern nearly two hundred years ago is sometimes still seen there, as are strange occurrences like lanterns that glow without being lit.

CHAPTER 4   Manassas National Battlefield Park
(Prince William County)   29

Site of the first major battle of the Civil War, ghosts of fallen soldiers have long been seen roaming the fields where they fell during the bloodiest conflict in U.S. history.

CHAPTER 5   Historic Occoquan (Occoquan)   35

This charming waterfront village is reportedly home to a number of ghosts, including a murdered Indian who haunts a restaurant and whose likeness has been seen in the restaurant's chimney smoke as well as in the mirror of the ladies' restroom.

CHAPTER 6   Rippon Lodge (Woodbridge) 43

The oldest house still standing in Prince William County, this tragic lodge was the scene of more than one murder, and spirits who should have moved on to another world, are said to linger there.

CHAPTER 7   Weems-Botts Museum (Dumfries) 49

Originally the home of Mason Locke Weems, who fabricated the story of George Washington and the cherry tree, this site is now a museum and is said to be haunted by the ghosts of two sisters who both lived their lives in misery there.

CENTRAL 59

CHAPTER 8   Berry Hill Road (Pittsylvania County)   60

Creepy under ideal conditions, this seven-and-a-half mile stretch of road and the surrounding areas are home to ghosts, abandoned farmsteads, blighted woodlands, gravitational anomalies, and "Satan's Bridge."

CHAPTER 9   Civil War Hospital Museum Exchange Hotel (Gordonsville)   67

Once a hotel that served as a battlefield hospital during the Civil War, this site is now a museum that is said to house the spirits of soldiers who died from their wounds during the bloody conflict.

CHAPTER 10   Edgar Allan Poe Museum (Richmond)   73

Not far from where Edgar Allan Poe lived and worked, this museum is located in a historic house and contains a shrine to the troubled American author. Though the museum's curator is skeptical, others have seen evidence of hauntings, including prankish ghosts who pinch and toss things at visitors.

CHAPTER 11   Trapezium House (Petersburg)   80

This house contains no parallel walls, having been so constructed according to the guidance of a West Indian servant who advised that building it in this way would ward off evil spirits. According to some, however, the house is nonetheless haunted by the ghosts of former inhabitants.

CHAPTER 12   Wreck of the Old 97 (Danville)   87

Immortalized in the first recorded song to sell a million copies in the United States, the Southern Express train No. 97 plummeted into a ravine in 1903, killing eleven people and injuring seven others on board. The ghosts associated with its story, however, may not be those of people who were actually on the train.

COAST 95

CHAPTER 13   Assateague Lighthouse (Assateague Island)   96

Assateague Island's rich history, rugged coastline, and population of wild horses is interesting enough, but the lighthouse, which was originally constructed in 1867 and later rebuilt, is said to be haunted by its former keeper and perhaps Spanish sailors who drowned near the islands's shores.

CHAPTER 14   1848 Island Manor House
(Chincoteague Island)   104

Built by two affluent professionals in 1848 as an impressive manor house, this home played an important role during the Civil War and is today the most historic B&B on Chincoteague. No fewer than three ghosts are believed to haunt its chambers.

CHAPTER 15   Colonial Williamsburg (Williamsburg)   113

One of the oldest municipalities in the United States, Colonial Williamsburg is the site of numerous 18th-century buildings said to be haunted by ghosts—a female ghost who fled a party, losing one shoe along the way, another female ghost who was hit by a speeding carriage, and even George Washington himself (or is that just another man in a wig and frock coat?).

CHAPTER 16   Fort Monroe (Hampton)   121

In continuous usage by U.S. military forces for more than 170 years, this coastal redoubt is the site of several hauntings and could be the inspiration for Edgar Allan Poe's story, "The Cask of Amontillado."

MOUNTAIN 131

CHAPTER 17   Barter Theatre (Abingdon)   132

Opened during the Great Depression, this theatre allowed people in the isolated town of Abingdon to trade homegrown produce for tickets to live entertainment. It is believed by some to be home to the ghost of its founder, and has a "Scary Room" that puts actors on edge to this day.

CHAPTER 18   Carroll County Courthouse (Hillsville)   140

In 1912, a murderous spree at the conclusion of a trial claimed the lives of five people, including the sheriff and presiding judge. The site of those attacks, the Carroll County Courthouse, is believed by some to be haunted by the spirits of the slain, forever searching for justice.

CHAPTER 19   Devil's Den (Fancy Gap)   149

This cold, damp cave in the Blue Ridge Mountains has a history as a hiding place—perhaps for the Underground Railway and also for some of the gunmen in the 1912 shooting at the nearby Carroll County Courthouse. It is also definitely the site of multiple unquiet spirits.

CHAPTER 20   Octagon House (Marion)   157

This crumbling brick edifice, built in the shape of an octagon, was home to slave-owner Abijah Thomas, who is said to haunt the place every December 1; and many say the spirits of his tortured slaves haunt it too.

CHAPTER 21   U.S. Route 58 (Lee, Scott, Washington, Grayson, Carroll, and Patrick Counties)   164

While it may not be actually haunted itself, the western stretch of Route 58—a mountainous road that runs along Virginia's southern boundary—goes through numerous ghost hamlets and is a useful thoroughfare for those hunting for haunted sites in this most isolated part of the Old Dominion.

VALLEY   175

CHAPTER 22   Belle Grove Plantation (Middletown)   176

Once a grain and livestock farm, today Belle Grove Plantation is a tourist site. But watch out for the ghost of Hetty Cooley, who was reportedly brutally murdered by one of her husband's slaves.

CHAPTER 23   Cedar Creek Battlefield (Frederick, Shenandoah, and Warren Counties)   184

This battlefield has been the site of numerous apparitions in the years since one of the Civil War's bloodiest battles was fought on it.

CHAPTER 24   Poor House Road Tunnel (Rockbridge County)   188

Local legends have branded this out-of-the-way tunnel as the site of horrible events in the past. Various ghosthunting expeditions have collected evidence that it might, indeed, be haunted by troubled spirits.

CHAPTER 25   Virginia Military Institute (Lexington)   194

Often called the West Point of the South, VMI has a wealth of ghost lore

associated with it, including a weeping statue, a mural with moving figures, and
the sounds of ghostly cannon fire.

CHAPTER 26   Ghosts of the Valley (Winchester)   202

This town at the northern end of the Shenandoah Valley may very well be the
state's most haunted city, and includes numerous sites with haunted histories.
These include the Fuller House Inn, the Union Bank, the Cork Street Tavern,
Mount Hebron Cemetery, and virtually every historic building along its
pedestrian mall.

CHAPTER 27   Wayside Inn (Middletown)   216

For more than 210 years, this inn in the heart of Virginia has catered to the needs
of travelers. Visitors and staff members alike have had numerous experiences
with the ghosts that have remained behind in its storied rooms.

DISTRICT OF COLUMBIA   223

CHAPTER 28   America's Greatest Haunted City
(Washington, D.C.)   224

An overview of haunted sites in the nation's capital reveals it to be a city rife with
ghosts and places where inexplicable events have been known to occur.

CHAPTER 29   Decatur House (Washington, D.C.)   233

Located near the White House on Lafayette Square, this two-hundred-year-old
house was tainted by slavery and untimely death and is reputed to be one of the
most haunted places in the capital city.

CHAPTER 30   Ford's Theatre (Washington, D.C.)   243

Ever since President Abraham Lincoln was assassinated here by actor John Wilkes
Booth while attending a showing of *Our American Cousin,* this small, historic
theatre has been the site of strange sightings and occurrences.

Visiting Haunted Places   253

Ghostly Resources   265

Acknowledgments   269

About the Author   271

Welcome to America's Haunted Road Trip

DO YOU BELIEVE IN GHOSTS?

If you're like 52 percent of Americans (according to a recent Harris Poll), you *do* believe that ghosts walk among us. Perhaps you've heard your name called in a dark and empty house. It could be that you have awoken to the sound of footsteps outside your bedroom door, only to find no one there. It is possible that you saw your grandmother sitting in her favorite rocking chair, the same grandmother who passed away several years before. Maybe you took a photo of a crumbling, deserted farmhouse and discovered strange mists and orbs in the photo, anomalies that were not visible to your naked eye.

If you have experienced similar paranormal events, then you know that ghosts exist. Even if you have not yet experienced these things, you're curious about the paranormal world, the spirit realm. If you weren't, you wouldn't be reading this preface to the latest book in the America's Haunted Road Trip series from Clerisy Press.

Over the last several years, I've investigated haunted locations across the country and with each new site, I found myself becoming more fascinated by ghosts. What are they? How do they manifest themselves? Why are they here? These are just a few of the questions I've been asking. No doubt, you've been asking the same questions.

You'll find some answers to those questions when you take America's Haunted Road Trip. We've gathered some of America's top ghost writers (no pun intended) and researchers to explore their states' favorite haunts. Each location is open to the public so you can visit them yourself and try out your ghosthunting skills. In addition to telling you about their often hair-raising adventures, the writers include maps and travel directions to guide your own haunted road trip.

It is said that "Virginia is for lovers," but Mike Varhola's *Ghosthunting Virginia* proves that the state is fertile ground for ghosthunters as well. The book is a spine-tingling trip through Virginia's sleepy small towns and historic sites, with a side trip to the District of Columbia thrown in for good measure. Ride shotgun with Mike as he seeks out Civil War ghosts at the Cedar Creek and Manassas battlefields. Travel with him to Belle Grove Plantation in Middletown where the ghost of the murdered Hetty Cooley still roams the house that was once hers. And who belongs to the disembodied voices that whisper in the Poor House Road Tunnel in Rockbridge County? Hang on tight; *Ghosthunting Virginia* is a scary ride.

But once you've finished reading this book, don't unbuckle your seatbelt. There are still forty-nine states left for your haunted road trip! See you on the road!

John Kachuba
Editor, America's Haunted Road Trip

Ghosthunting Virginia

AMERICA'S
HAUNTED ROAD TRIP

Introduction

WELCOME TO *Ghosthunting Virginia!*

When I was asked to write this book, my editors knew me to be an established author of nonfiction books; to have a strong background in history, research, and fieldwork; and to live in Virginia and just outside of Washington, D.C. They had no reason to believe I've had an abiding interest in the paranormal for some thirty years. Nor, indeed, could they have known that I had been a "ghosthunter" some years before that term would have meant anything to most people.

Since moving to Virginia in 1991, I had not spent much time contemplating whether it was a particularly haunted state, much less undertaken nearly as many ghosthunting expeditions as I would have liked. My interests in such subjects had largely been subordinated by school, work, and family, and the unseen world I had once relished exploring was out of sight and, increasingly, out of mind. So, when I had the opportunity to turn my attentions to it once again through this book, I eagerly accepted.

Two years after I arrived in the Old Dominion, there occurred something that moved my interest in the paranormal from the realm of the esoteric into that of the mainstream: *The X Files*. There had been television shows and plenty of movies about the paranormal before this nine-season program—my favorite being *Kolchak: The Night Stalker*—but nothing before had been quite as successful or universally known. Though the show's success probably was due in part to our culture's increasing interest in the topics the show explored, I suspect that other shows about ghosthunting and similar esoteric subjects would not have been as popular in its absence.

My own affinity for the show stemmed from my longstanding interest in the supernatural, which lay not dead but dreaming within me, and I never lost my awareness that there are innumerable things in this world beyond the realm of the mundane. My guiding principal has long been that incisive phrase spoken by Hamlet to his friend Horatio (while holding a skull, no less).

"There are more things in heaven and earth," Shakespeare wrote, "Than are dreamt of in your philosophy." In short, there are countless things in this world that cannot be adequately explained by any single conventional system of beliefs.

Despite an ongoing awareness of the unseen world and knowledge of things like the ghost tours held in historic Virginia towns such as Alexandria, Fairfax, and Winchester, I was surprised to discover upon starting to research this project just how many haunted sites there are in the state and adjacent Washington, D.C. To say that this book could have a hundred chapters devoted to publicly accessible haunted sites would be a marked understatement, and to say that it could have a thousand if private venues were also included would not be inaccurate. Distilling all of the possible choices into a mere thirty chapters was not the smallest challenge associated with this project.

Suffice it to say, Virginia and the District of Columbia are fertile ground for ghosthunters and have no shortage of potential venues for investigation. And I have spared no efforts to make this guidebook as useful a resource as possible for those interested in visiting haunted sites.

In any event, my goal with this book has not been to prove or convince anyone that any of the places I visited are indeed haunted. It has been, rather, to identify sites that have ghostly phenomena associated with them, visit them, and compile their history and my experiences into a book that other people with an interest in the subject could use as a guide for their own visits. That said, I am willing to go on the record as saying that I believe any of the sites covered in this book could be haunted and am firmly convinced that at least five of them certainly are. Which those are I will leave to readers to determine for themselves.

Ghosthunting as a pursuit has certainly come into its own over the past few years, and it and associated phenomena have become the subjects of numerous television shows and movies. In my experience, however, real ghosthunting bears very little resemblance to what is depicted even in "reality" shows related to the subject. The real thing is generally much less manic, a lot quieter, and—despite the absence of noise, running back and forth, and jerky camera angles—much more intense. It also does not result in evidence of haunting on every expedition.

Many ghosthunters today use a wide variety of electronic equipment, and there can certainly be some value associated with this approach. I do not believe, however, anyone should hesitate to engage in ghosthunting based on a lack of equipment, and am myself more of a "naturalistic" ghosthunter. For various reasons, I use a minimum of equipment in my investigations and not much more than I have ever used as a writer and reporter: a microcassette recorder, a digital camera, a pen and notepad, and a flashlight. I have also found a full tank of gas and some food and water to be useful when heading into relatively isolated areas.

I also think a ghosthunter's innate senses are just as critical to an investigation as any sort of equipment. While I make no claims here to be a "psychic investigator," I do believe that most people have access to certain paranormal senses that they can draw upon if they choose to and are aware of them. People who can use such abilities reliably, of course, have generally spent many years honing them and learning to differentiate exterior phenomena from internal thoughts. People without such experience should probably err on the side of caution and in the absence of corroborating evidence assume that whatever they are "sensing" could very well be a product of their imaginations.

While investigating Devil's Den in southwestern Virginia, for example, I came virtually face to face with what I believe to have been a spirit entity of some sort and had the distinct impression of an Indian shaman. While it is a pretty sure bet that this site was, indeed, visited and possibly even used by Indians, I have no actual evidence to support this supposition, and am thus not willing to accept as a true psychic impression.

Beyond experience, a good attitude is crucial. While the following chapters include a lot of information that can be useful when visiting the specific sites, there is one bit of general advice I would like offer to prospective ghosthunters: show respect for both the rights of any relevant living people (i.e., property owners) and for the dignity of any spirits that might be lingering at a particular site. I believe that ghosthunting is an endeavor fraught with its own potential hazards, and my sense is that anyone who acts inappropriately for too long is ultimately going to suffer some unhappy consequences—whether legal, spiritual, or otherwise.

For a good example of what *not* to do, check out a recent episode of the British ghosthunting show *Most Haunted*, during which the cast visited a purportedly haunted shipyard named Cammell Laird. Especially appalling was the behavior of the female host, who kept snapping orders at any ghosts that might have been present. Members of the crew said demeaning things about them, and a narrator made reference to "goading" ghosts into revealing themselves. The capacity of ghosts to visit various misfortunes upon people is limited, but if it is at all possible to call them down on oneself, this sort of behavior is probably the way to do it. Beyond that, people who act this way are creeps.

Determining exactly what ghosts are is beyond the scope

of this book, and throughout it terms like "ghost," "phantasm," "specter," and "spirit" are used fairly synonymously and are not intended as technical terms indicating manifestations with specific and differing characteristics. This is, after all, primarily a travel guide, not a tome devoted to the classification of earth-bound spirits, which would be of little practical use to most readers.

That said, the term "ghosts" runs the gamut from nonsentient residues of spiritual energy that can be detected by various means, to intelligent manifestations that can make their presences felt in various ways. My sense is that the vast majority of hauntings are of the lower order and that it is quite possible to have subtly haunted sites that are never identified as such due to a lack of investigation.

All of the places described in this book are believed to be haunted. Some people were quite forthcoming about discussing haunted places while others were more tight-lipped for whatever reasons.

One thing I have encountered while investigating potentially haunted places is the phenomena commonly known as "orbs," which are sometimes captured in digital photographs. No one can be involved with ghosthunting for too long without stumbling across the ongoing debate over these spherical objects and what they might be. Some people believe orbs are manifestations of spiritual energy. Others—including many veteran ghosthunters—dismiss these phenomena for a various reasons, a common one being that orbs are nothing more than a byproduct of low-light photography and represent an improperly developed spot on an image.

I am definitely of the former school of thought. In short, in the years since I have been using a digital camera, I have taken tens of thousands of pictures under all sorts of conditions. Of all those pictures, the only ones that have displayed orbs are ones I took at fewer than a half dozen locations, all of them reputed to be haunted. To me, these phenomena are compelling evidence of what I believe to be some sort of spiritual energy and a hallmark of haunted sites.

But the point of this book is not for me to convince anybody of anything. It is, rather, to provide a tool that prospective ghosthunters can use to help them find haunted sites, conduct their own investigations, and draw their own conclusions. I wish you the best of luck and look forward to hearing from you as you conduct your own visits to the sites listed in this book!

Michael J. Varhola
Springfield, Virginia
July 2008

NORTHERN

Maryland

LOUDOUN

Washington, D.C.

FAIRFAX

ARLINGTON

PRINCE
WILLIAM

STAFFORD

VIRGINIA:
NORTHERN AREA

Alexandria
  Gadsby's Tavern

Arlington
  Abingdon Plantation
  Arlington Cemetery

Clifton
  Bunny Man Bridge

Dumfries
  Weems-Botts Museum

Manassas
  Manassas National Battlefield
  Park

Occoquan
  Historic Occoquan

Woodbridge
  Rippon Lodge

7

CHAPTER 1

Arlington National Cemetery
ARLINGTON

*We are met on a great battlefield ... We have come to dedicate
a portion of that field, as a final resting place for those who
here gave their lives that that nation might live. ... But, in a
larger sense, we can not dedicate—we can not consecrate—
we can not hallow—this ground. The brave men, living and
dead, who struggled here, have consecrated it, far above our
poor power to add or detract.*

—Abraham Lincoln, "Gettysburg Address"

ARLINGTON NATIONAL CEMETERY is a necropolis,
a city of the dead, in the truest sense, and in its 640 acres rest

more than 320,000 U.S. military service personnel and their spouses. If it were a city of the living, it would be the 57th largest in the country, falling right in between Cincinnati, Ohio, and Bakersfield, California. There is, in fact, only one U.S. military cemetery that is larger—Long Island National Cemetery—and not by much, with somewhat more than 329,000 internments as of this writing. As an active cemetery, Arlington's population of souls—resting in peace and unquiet alike—is constantly growing and, on average, some twenty-seven funerals are conducted at the cemetery every weekday

Arlington National Cemetery clings to a wooded, riverside stretch of the Virginia hills across the Potomac from Washington, D.C., its main entrance being directly adjacent to the Lincoln Memorial. It is the final resting place for veterans of all of America's military conflicts, from the Revolutionary War up through the current and ongoing actions in Afghanistan and Iraq (from which the number of internments steadily grows). Hundreds of the nation's most famous veterans are buried at the site, including Audie Murphy, Creighton Abrams, Gregory "Pappy" Boyington, Omar Bradley, Joe Louis, Glenn Miller, John F. Kennedy, and Phillip Sheridan.

It was during the Civil War that the cemetery was opened—veterans of earlier wars being moved there after 1900—and the site was originally part of the 1,100-acre Arlington Mansion plantation. This estate was, in fact, the property of Mary Anna Custis Lee, the wife of Confederate military commander Robert E. Lee and the granddaughter of Martha Washington. As casualties from the protracted insurrection grew into the tens of thousands, however, the federal government needed new cemeteries for them, and Union leaders decided that the grounds of the rebel leader's home would be both convenient and appropriate.

"The grounds about the mansion are admirably adapted to such a use," wrote U.S. Army Quartermaster General Montgomery C. Meigs in his recommendation that the estate be confiscated for this use. His suggestion was heartily approved, and on May 13, 1864, Private William Henry Christman of the 67th Pennsylvania Infantry became the first military serviceman to be interred in Arlington National Cemetery—about a month before the site was officially designated as a military cemetery. He was followed over the next year or so by another 16,000 of his brothers-in-arms.

Not everyone was happy about this, of course, and the members of the Custis family, of which Lee's wife was a scion, were enraged by it. They would not have been in favor of killing so many Yankee soldiers if they had liked them in the first place, and having their home turned into a cemetery for them seemed like a deliberate affront. By all accounts it was, and Union soldiers were buried right in Mrs. Lee's rose garden and her home turned into a headquarters for the superintendent of the cemetery.

Once the rule of law was reestablished in the wake of the failed Southern rebellion, the Lee family took full advantage of it. Eight years after the war ended, Robert E. Lee's son, George Washington Custis Lee, a Confederate general in his own right, sued the government and, after a prolonged case that ultimately reached the U.S. Supreme Court, had title to the property returned to his family. Not wanting to live at an estate on which 16,000 of his enemies and 3,800 freed slaves were buried and whose ghosts would doubtless have tormented him and his family in perpetuity, he sold the title back to the U.S. government for $150,000, securing its role as a national cemetery.

Today, the house, along with the outbuildings and grounds immediately surrounding it are maintained and operated by the National Park Service, which now dubs it the "Robert E. Lee Memorial" as a gesture of reconciliation between the two halves of the once-divided country. Nearby Memorial Bridge, linking the cemetery with the Lincoln Memorial, park service guides tell visitors to the site, was designed as a symbol of this reunification.

Arlington National Cemetery itself is administered by the Department of the Army, which operates it on behalf of veterans of all the military services.

There is a line of thought expressed by some people that cemeteries are actually the least likely place in which to encounter ghosts. This is presumably based on the idea that all of the people interred within a cemetery have been properly buried with all appropriate ceremony and there is thus no good reason for their spirits to be unquiet. This does not really make much more sense to me than making generalizations about the inhabitants of cities of the living in general and presumes the people most unhappy about the ways they died will be mollified by a few words and a burial plot. Furthermore, that theory does not seem to be borne out by prevailing evidence in general, and not at all by Arlington National Cemetery in particular.

Arlington National Cemetery has, in fact, come to have a great deal of ghostly phenomena associated with it since it was founded. Curiously, many of these phenomena are distinctly positive in nature, but perhaps that is not so strange in a place where so many who have given their lives for their country are laid to rest.

One of the places within the cemetery where people are said to have felt a spiritual presence is the grave of Robert F. Kennedy, who is buried near his brother, President John F. Kennedy. Singer Bobby Darin, one of the mourners at the slain senator's June 1968 funeral, is the first to have made this claim. Darin said he felt compelled to remain at the gravesite after the service and that he was thereafter swathed in a bright light that coalesced into a ball of energy and then passed through and "emotionally cleansed" him. He maintained subsequently that Kennedy's spirit had reached out to him and that his life was changed for the better as a result. Other people have since reported similar incidents at both of the Kennedy gravesites.

A similar kind of effect has been reported in the vicinity

The grave of John F. Kennedy

of the Tomb of the Unknowns—originally known as the Tomb of the Unknown Soldier but which is now the resting place for three unidentified dead—where some people have claimed to feel what has been characterized as a "vortex of etheric energy." This energy, according to people who have experienced it at various locations around the tomb, is supposed to have the effect of physical, mental, and spiritual regeneration.

But the area within the national cemetery that has had the most evidence of haunting associated with it—and not of a positive nature—is Arlington Mansion itself. The 8,000-square-foot, neoclassical plantation house has long been purported to be haunted by the ghosts of the Lee and Custis family members who were forced to relinquish it as their home as a result of the Civil War.

"The security people won't go in the house at night unless they have to," a National Park Service guide I spoke with at the site told me in July 2008. Things they and other guides have experienced in and around the house, he said, include the sound of disembodied footsteps, especially on stairways; the sound of crying babies in the middle of the night; and the smell of perfume in the rooms formerly occupied by female members of the family. Almost all of the incidents, he said, have occurred during hours of darkness.

Robert E. Lee himself is one of the ghosts believed by some to haunt the mansion, and people have reported seeing or otherwise sensing his specter in the years since the Arlington Mansion estate was confiscated by the government. This should actually be a bit surprising when one considers how Lee is generally regarded by people in North and South alike today. After all, the spirits of heroes who believe they have done the right thing have little inducement to lurk about after death making things go bump in the night.

But the Lee familiar to most people today bears little resemblance to the real man, and is little more than a sentimentalized, two-dimensional construct created by maudlin writers who treat the worst event ever to strike the United States as if it were some golden age. In reality, Robert E. Lee had grave reservations about the legitimacy of the Southern cause and his role in it, as evidenced by his own writings, and knew that he was a traitor to his country, the oaths of military service he made before God, even his own father.

"Our national independence, and consequently our individual liberty," wrote Revolutionary War hero Henry "Lighthorse Harry" Lee, father of Robert E. Lee, in 1799. "Our peace and our happiness depend entirely on maintaining our union. In point of right no state can withdraw itself from the union. In point of policy, no state ought to be permitted to do so." Robert E. Lee did everything he could to destroy the legacy his father had struggled to create and in which he had so fervently believed.

And maybe it is the fact that Lee has been so mischaracter-
ized, that he has been made into a sort of hero and the home
where he lived turned into a memorial to him, that has led to
his haunting the site—not because it is the home where he once
lived, but because it is surrounded by the graves of men who he
knows would likely never have been killed in a bloody civil war
if he had been true to his country, his word, and the ideals of
his forebears. He will likely never rest while people continue to
invoke his name and treat him as something he did not believe
himself to be.

Arlington National Cemetery has always had somewhat of
an otherworldly feel to me, and I have little doubt that it is, in
fact, a haunt for spirits, of both those who have betrayed their
country and those who have given all they had in its service.
Whether a visitor senses a negative presence or a positive one
while visiting the site will depend on which they happen to
encounter and, possibly, to the spirit with which they approach
this most hallowed site.

CHAPTER 2

Bunny Man Bridge
FAIRFAX STATION

Over the years the story has evolved into a ghost story suit-able for parties, camp outs, and any occasion that such tales are exchanged. It was at one such gathering in 1976 that [I] first heard it told.... I never saw the Bunny Man myself, but then I never strayed into the woods at night, especially not near the bridge ....

—Brian A. Conley, "The Bunny Man Unmasked:
The Real Life Origins of an Urban Legend"

FOR THE PAST SEVENTEEN YEARS, I have lived about eight miles from what some people have claimed is not just

one of the most haunted sites in the country but, according to a
2001 episode of one television show, one of "The Scariest Places
on Earth." Tens of thousands of people live within that radius
of it in densely populated Fairfax County, so there is nothing
strange there. What I found to be uncanny, however, was that
I had never even heard about it until my friend Geoff Weber
asked me in late 2007 if it was one of the sites I was planning
to cover in this book.

I forgot that conversation until May 2008, when I stumbled
across a reference to Bunny Man Bridge online, followed by several more when I started to poke around a bit. At that point I
resolved to visit it as part of my fieldwork for this book and to ask
Geoff—who is, among other things, a professional magician—
if he wanted to accompany me. After all, I figured, it couldn't
hurt to have someone with ostensible influence over the spirit
world along on a venture of this sort. And, as he had told me
about the site, it seemed doubly appropriate.

A bit of online research prior to our visit yielded a number of
Web sites with information about the site, including suggestions
that the Bunny Man legend may have even influenced scenes in
at least one movie, *Donnie Darko,* and one video game, "Manhunt." I found one of these sources—a detailed essay called
"The Bunny Man Unmasked"—to be especially significant and
unique in a particular way, and not just because it was longer,
more detailed, and better written than most. It was written by
Brian A. Conley, a historian-archivist with the Fairfax County
Public Library system and appears on the section of the Fairfax County government Web site devoted to that organization.
This article is, in short, the only material I have found from a
governmental source that addresses a possibly haunted site, and
the legend behind it, in any sort of a substantive way (the official
"Virginia is for Lovers" Web site mentions many sites, but only
in a peripheral or inaccurate way).

The roots of the legend are supposed to date as far back as 1908, and it has verifiably been told in the Washington, D.C., area since at least the early 1970s. These tales generally tell of a maniac dressed in a bunny suit, armed with an appropriate weapon (e.g., axe, chain saw, butcher knife), who slays wayward adolescents who cross his path in the course of their disobedience. Perhaps predictably, the killer is often said to be an escapee from an insane asylum, sometimes cited as the Southwestern Virginia Mental Health Institute in the Virginia mountain town of Marion. Animal mutilations are among the additional crimes typically attributed to him.

Bunny Man stories have been set as far south as Culpepper and some versions have spread into Washington, D.C., itself and the adjacent Maryland counties. Year after year, however, the stories consistently come back to the same site, a railway overpass that is widely referred to as Bunny Man Bridge.

A great many of the online references to the bridge are devoted to debunking the legend of the Bunny Man himself. Whether the story is true or not, however, has nothing to do with whether the site is actually haunted. It is certainly possible, for example, that people might have sensed or come to realize that the bridge was haunted and, in the absence of any better explanation, created or appropriated the existing Bunny Man story for these purposes. My desire was not to confirm or refute the urban myth itself but to investigate the site to which it is commonly linked and see if it warrants attention from ghosthunters.

Bunny Man Bridge is often described in online accounts as being in Clifton. When I attempted to run directions from my home to Colchester Road in Clifton, however, the resulting map showed a short, deadend spur of a road that did not cross a railway track. When I ran directions to Colchester Road in Fairfax Station, on the other hand, the map showed me a four- or five-mile-long, north-south road that crossed a railway track near its southern end.

Directions aside, I was pretty much expecting Geoff to serve as our guide during the excursion we planned for the night of June 3, 2008, and to draw upon his memories of the nighttime automotive rambles that had led him to the bridge as a high-schooler. And, when he showed up at my house around 9:30 P.M. on that night, he was armed with a handheld GPS unit to reinforce his possibly fuzzy memories of those visits to the bridge more than a decade before.

Unfortunately, I had not passed on to Geoff what I had learned when running directions to the site, and we did not go far up darkened Colchester Road before it ended in someone's driveway and I realized he had keyed it in as a Clifton location. He reprogrammed the unit, and we followed our new directions, which guided us through the historic town of Clifton and to the Fairfax Station leg of the road.

I distinctly remembered my directions showing a right-hand turn onto the road, so that is the direction we went. It did not seem to get more isolated or creepier, however, and after a few miles Geoff said something did not seem right. After another mile or so the road ended at the intersection with an unmarked highway, and we realized we must have somehow gone the wrong direction. As we turned around and headed back down Colchester Road the way we had just come, both of us reflected that the evening was starting to feel an awful lot like a scene from *The Blair Witch Project*, and I started to wonder whether we were actually going to find the bridge at all.

"So how do you tell if a place you visit is haunted?" Geoff asked me as we worked our way back up the dark country road.

"Well, there are a lot of ways to tell if it might be haunted" I replied slowly while considering my answer. "Sometimes it is a gradual sort of thing and comes to you at a point after you get home and download and look at your photos, listen to your audio tape, and think over what you experienced. Your mind correlates all the different pieces and a shiver goes up the back of your neck as it just sort of dawns on you that you have spent time in a place that is occupied by ghosts."

As we passed the point where we turned the wrong way, I realized the mistake I had made, which was based on having approached Colchester Road from the direction opposite from that I had thought. It was, indeed, getting creepier looking, and as the road bore to the left ahead of us, we saw the light-colored concrete of the bridge appear in the darkness. Bunny Man Bridge is not, in fact, really a bridge at all. From our perspective, it was actually a tunnel, and even from the perspective of train traffic it was not a load-bearing structure over a gap but merely a means of allowing road traffic to pass through the railway embankment.

With nowhere safe-looking to park near the north side of the structure, we drove on through it, went up to a spot where we could turn around, and parked at the left side of the road a few hundred feet from the bridge. We then got out of the car, collected our camera, recorder, and flashlights, and moved toward the bridge to examine it.

Graffiti is a perennial concern for the authorities in Fairfax County and, while Geoff remembered the bridge as being rife with such markings in the past, it had been all but stripped of them when we visited. One set of relatively fresh markings near the north entrance was all that we could see as we passed through one end of the one-hundred-foot-long tunnel and out the other.

We took a number of photos and then headed back through to the side where we had parked. It occurred to me at that point that one of the legends linked with the Bunny Man is nearly identical to those associated with "Bloody Mary" stories and movies like *Candyman*, namely that uttering his name three

times while at the bridge will cause him to either appear or otherwise make his presence known. Geoff said he had heard that
story as well, and proceeded to make the threefold invocation,
pausing between the first and second utterances to ask me what
was supposed to happen.

As he finished saying the name for the third time, I was
stunned to see a glow appear in the tunnel! It was followed a
few seconds later by a Crown Victoria sedan. As it passed by
our vehicle, its rack of piercing blue lights began to flash, and it
flipped a U-turn and then parked. Its door opened, and a police
officer got out.

"So, did you see him?" she said.

"Nope," I replied. "My friend said 'Bunny Man' three times,
but then you appeared."

"Well, maybe I'm the Bunny Man," she said. I responded by
telling her that I certainly hoped she didn't have a set of rabbit
ears and a chain saw in her police cruiser.

She was, in fact, Fairfax County Police Officer Kathryn
Schroth, who told us that this was a popular spot for kids to
smoke pot, and asked if we were carrying any. We said we
weren't, and explained our presence at the bridge. We chatted
with her a few minutes and said we were planning on taking a
few more pictures and then leaving. She said we looked "legit"
and, after warning us to keep off the embankment itself and
the private property at either side of the road, left us to our
business.

Geoff and I decided to both try invoking the Bunny Man
again, my sense being that interrupting the sequence to say
something else might have invalidated the process. (Note that
when I see people do things like this in movies I think they
are pretty stupid to invite whatever hazards might be associated
with such a ritual, but Geoff suggested that legitimate research
made it okay).

Nothing seemed to happen. We walked back toward the car and got ready to leave.

Geoff got in the car before me, and, as I opened the driver's side door to get in, I looked at the bridge once more. I took one more picture of it, and as I did, I heard the distinct snap of a branch in the woods just to my left.

"I think we've overstayed our welcome," I said half-jokingly, and got in the car. We drove through the bridge, back up Colchester Road, and then home.

Other than the feeling of disquiet I had at the very end of our visit to Bunny Man Bridge, I did not get a sense that the site was much more than a place for kids to toke up and for cops to keep an eye on. So when I got home around 11:30 and downloaded my photos, I did not expect that any of them would reveal anything out of the ordinary. And on that account, I was very wrong.

Of the fifty-four pictures I took, more than twenty were simply black, revealing nothing, and about half of the others looked as if they had some merit. Two, however, were significant.

One, taken from the north end of the tunnel, showed at the left of the entrance a very clear, solid-looking, pale blue-green orb of the sort that is frequently taken by ghosthunters to be a manifestation of spiritual energy.

The other was even stranger. It was that last shot I had taken from the south end of the tunnel and showed a whole array of orbs in a variety of sizes that looked as if they were converging on the spot where I was standing. Most of these electronic phenomena were not very resilient, and when I zoomed in on them too much they broke up and became indistinguishable from foliage and other background elements: I probably would have just dismissed them as drops of moisture on my lens if any of my other shots had displayed similar effects. One of them, however, looked very strange to me and was, in fact, unlike any other sort of orb I had ever seen, and so *like* something else that it made me shudder. I resolved to show it to my wife the next day to see if she would see the same thing I had.

The following day, I asked Diane to take a look at the two images in which I had picked up the anomalies.

"That's an orb," she said confidently after scanning the first image and quickly spotting the detail in question. She moved on to the other one, noting the odd, pale orbs and then focusing on the one that had caught my attention.

"It's a face!" she said, and that shudder ran across my back again, tingling even my face and scalp. And that is, in fact, what it looked like. More substantial than the others, it appeared to be about ten or twelve feet off the ground and to be about the size of a human head. When we zoomed in on it just enough—but not so much it began to pixilate—it looked like a small, pallid face, complete with eyes, nose, mouth, and ears.

Since then, I have opened that photo a few more times, but not often. That is because it bothers me to look at it and because it seems to me that something—the Bunny Man, or whatever it is that haunts that bridge so close to my home—had, in fact, apparently come in answer to our summons and made its presence known to us.

CHAPTER 3

Gadsby's Tavern
ALEXANDRIA

To the memory of a Female Stranger, whose mortal suffering terminated on the 4th day of October, 1816.

This stone is erected by her disconsolate husband in whose arms she sighed out her latest breath, and who under God did his utmost to soothe the cold dull hour of death.

How loved, how honor'd once avails the not, to whom related or by whom begot, a heap of dust remains of thee 'tis all thou art, and all the proud shall be.

—Inscription on a tombstone
in St. Paul's Cemetery, Alexandria

ESTABLISHED AROUND 1785, Gadsby's Tavern has been a quintessential Alexandria watering hole throughout most of U.S. history. And, as with most places over a certain age, it has a number of ghost stories associated with it and is one of the stops on local ghost tours.

Today, Alexandria is probably most distinguished as the home of more trade, professional, and nonprofit associations than any other city in the country, with the possible exception of nearby Washington, D.C., which is located just across the Potomac River. In the early years of the republic, however, especially prior to the founding of the capitol city, Alexandria was a vibrant port city, and Gadsby's Tavern played host to many of the most important people in the country. George Washington celebrated his birthday at the tavern in 1797 and 1798; Thomas Jefferson held his inaugural banquet there in 1801; and the tavern served as a hub of political, business, and social interaction for many years.

Ironically, despite having lived less than seventeen miles from the tavern for more than two decades, I never found an opportunity to visit it before I started writing this book. Not until a cool, gloomy day in March 2008, after attending a luncheon in Old Town, did I actually ask for directions to the place and walk the four blocks to it from where I had been conducting my other business.

Gadsby's Tavern consists of two separate buildings and two separate establishments. One is a museum, located in an older, two-story building, and the other a restaurant, located on the ground floor of a three-story building built as an expansion to the original structure in 1792 (at the time dubbed the City Tavern and Hotel). Having just come from a dry event, my inclination was to visit the latter.

A number of stories about incorporeal spirits, rather than the liquid ones it has traditionally served, have developed about

Gadsby's Tavern, and I had heard a number of them over the years. The most famous involves a beautiful young woman who died at the establishment nearly two hundred years ago and whose specter is sometimes purportedly still seen there.

As a common version of the story goes, the young woman and her husband arrived at the port of Alexandria in October 1816 from points unknown. She was very ill and was taken to Gadsby's Tavern, where she received treatment from a doctor and a number of nurses. Despite their best efforts, however, she died on October 14. For reasons still unknown, her husband made everyone they had dealt with swear that they would never reveal her identity, had her buried in nearby St. Paul's Cemetery beneath a nameless tombstone, and, soon after disappeared without paying any of his bills, including $1,500 for the stone.

Since then, visitors have reported seeing the ghost of the "female stranger" standing near her headstone, wandering the halls of Gadsby's Tavern, or peering out its windows while holding a candle (and, possibly, awaiting the return of her apparently deadbeat husband). Explanations for who she is have included the ward of an aging English aristocrat who was accidentally slain by her lover, with whom she fled to America; the daughter of Aaron Burr, who gunned down Alexander Hamilton in a duel; and an orphan, separated from her three siblings at a young age, who inadvertently married her brother. Die nameless and leave bills behind and, specifics aside, the stories about you are pretty sure to be sordid.

Other ghost stories associated with the tavern are fairly typical of those associated with haunted sites in general, and include candles or lanterns that appear to be burning, but, upon examination, have not been recently lit.

Glancing at the upper-story windows of the buildings as I approached them, I did not see anything out of the ordinary.

The first thing I learned upon being greeted inside the

Gadsby's Tavern and Museum

entrance to the restaurant by a distinguished-looking older gentleman is that it is no longer traditional to drop in off the street
for just a cold one at the tavern—the norm being to partake
of a meal as well—and that I would be better served for those
purposes at a nearby Irish pub (of course!). Upon seeing my
disappointment, however, he graciously relented, showed me to
a two-person table in the dining room, and asked his waiter to
bring me a beer.

"Are you the manager?" I asked him.

"Sometimes," he replied somewhat cagily (demonstrating a
dry sense of humor that was revealed when I eventually obtained
his business card and read upon it the title "General Manager"),
and introduced himself as Paul Carbé. I introduced myself and
briefly explained my interest in his establishment.

"Oh, you want the museum next door," he said, crushing

any hopes I might have of encountering spectral spoor at his establishment. I decided to just enjoy my Gadsby's ale and the ambience of the place, which included wait staff dressed in garb reminiscent of the Colonial era, pewter place settings on the tables, and dark wood paneling that in some cases dates to 1792.

"That's original," Carbé said, indicating the wooden fireplace mantle in the first of several tidbits of information that he congenially bestowed upon me on his way back and forth from the back of the restaurant and the front, where he dutifully greeted everyone who came through the door. Eventually, however, he decided to bestow something more substantial upon me.

"Come with me," he said, and led me to the back of the restaurant and into its kitchen. There, he proceeded to tell me about three strange episodes that some would take for evidence of a ghostly presence—*all of which had occurred in the previous month!*

In the first, he said, one of his waitresses walked into the kitchen and asked if anyone knew where beverage napkins were. As if in response, a package of beverage napkins pitched off a nearby shelf and landed on the counter next to the stunned young woman.

The second incident took place in a dining room that had been set up for a dinner party. With no apparent cause or prompting from anyone, a spoon from one of the place settings slid off the table and clattered onto the floor.

And, in the third incident, three or four of the wait staff were working in the tavern after it had closed when they all distinctly heard a candle in the main dining room—where none of them were—being blown out.

As is the case with most ostensibly haunted sites, none of these incidents necessarily mean anything in and of themselves. Even when they are considered as elements in an ongoing pattern of similar incidents, they prove nothing. But they

do reinforce to those willing to acknowledge them that there is
more in this world that can easily be explained by most philoso-
phies, to paraphrase a famous playwright.

That was what I thought to myself, in any event, as I finished up my pint of ale and snapped a few more pictures of the
tavern. Collecting up my things, I thanked Mr. Carbé for his
helpfulness and stepped outside into a late afternoon that had
turned from gloom to drizzle.

Turning back toward Gadsby's Tavern as I walked away
from it, I looked up at some of the upper-story windows, hoping
I might catch a glimpse of the ghost of the "female stranger."
But I did not prolong my gaze. After all, if you stare at something long enough, you can end up seeing just about anything,
whether it is really there or not.

CHAPTER 4

Manassas National Battlefield Park

PRINCE WILLIAM COUNTY

A friend of mine does Civil War reenactments, and he was at Manassas, Va., while a tour guide was enlightening a group of little kids. "He was telling them about how the 5th New York Zouaves had been wiped out right near where they were standing at Second Manassas," my friend said. "He asked them if they knew what a Zouave uniform looked like," my friend went on, "and one little girl said they wore baggy red pants and blue jackets and funny red hats. When the guide asked how she knew that, she pointed to a cannon at the top of a nearby hill and said, 'One of them was standing up there.' "We looked, but nobody was there."

—Jim Goldsworthy, *Cumberland Times-News*

BACK IN THE 1990s when I was running *Living History* magazine, I heard any number of stories from Civil War reenactors about ghosts on the Manassas Battlefield, and, if memory serves, many of them described spectral formations glimpsed in the misty darkness of predawn. I also talked or corresponded with a couple of psychic researchers in those days, and they confirmed their impressions of lingering spiritual energies at the site of the first major clash between Union and Confederate forces.

It certainly makes sense that if any battlefield were haunted it would be Manassas. After all, it was the site of two bloody confrontations within the space of a year—the second one far larger than the first—and thus has a double layer of psychic trauma associated with it.

Like most Civil War battles, each of the ones fought at this location has two names, one bestowed by the North and one by the South, a convention that can cause some confusion for novice historians or those with only a casual interest in the subject. Union commanders usually named battles for the nearest rivers, streams, creeks, or "runs," while Confederate leaders generally named them for towns or railroad junctions. It is thus that the two battles fought at this site are variously known as the First Battle of Manassas and the Second Battle of Manassas for nearby Manassas Junction (a practice often adopted to this day by those sympathetic to the Rebel cause), and as First Battle of Bull Run and the Second Battle of Bull Run for a neighboring stream (the official names given them by the U.S. government). We will use the former term here not because of sympathies one way or the other but because it corresponds with the name of the park associated with it.

The First Battle of Manassas was fought July 21, 1861, by formations of enthusiastic, brightly uniformed volunteers who on both sides were confident that their opponents would turn and run and that they would that day witness the end of the war. Despite a favorable outlook for the 35,000-strong Union

forces early in the day, some 32,500 Confederate troops ultimately drove their opponents from the field in rout. Credit for
much of this victory has been accorded to Brigadier General
Thomas Jackson, who that day earned the *nom de guerre* "Stonewall." Both fledgling armies were left disorganized and blood-
ied, with Northern casualties of 460 killed, 1,124 wounded, and
1,312 missing or captured, and Southern casualties of 387 killed,
1,582 wounded, and 13 missing. Many illusions as to the nature
and duration of the war were shattered that day in the chaos,
fear, and death of combat.

The Second Battle of Manassas was fought August 28–30,
1862, between experienced armies that were considerably larger,
with some sixty-two thousand men clad in Union blue facing
fifty thousand in Confederate gray over an area of more than
five thousand acres. It concluded in a solid Southern victory,
taking the Confederacy to its high-water mark; the prospects
for the rebel cause would only become steadily bleaker over the
ensuing three years. Casualties far exceeded those of the earlier
battle, and for the Union were about ten thousand killed and
wounded and for the Confederacy about thirteen hundred killed
and seven thousand wounded.

It is little wonder then that so many ghost stories should be
associated with the place, especially in the decades since 1940,
when the park was officially established by the National Park
Service. These have been so widespread as to periodically catch
the attention of various local news organizations.

"Visitors ... have reported seeing house lights where there
is not a house, smelled the scent of black powder and once 'the
smell of burning flesh,'" reported the *Washington Post* in a 1989
article, for example. "Park employees have also testified to sudden drops in temperature on muggy days and baffling noises
in the battlefield Stone House." Any number of accounts of personal experiences, sightings, or investigations can be found in
numerous articles, books, and online postings.

Many of the most prolific and convincing ghost stories involve the 5th New York Volunteer Infantry regiment, dubbed "Duryée's Zouaves," a Union unit that in August 1862, according to historian Bruce Catton, "lost 117 men killed and 170 wounded, out of 490 present—the highest percentage of loss, in killed, suffered by any Federal regiment in one battle during the entire war." In the years especially since the park was established, many people have reported seeing one or more apparitions clad in the distinctive uniforms of this ill-fated formation at various locations in the park, especially near the monument dedicated to the fallen soldiers.

"There, at dusk, images of members of the 5th New York Zouaves—who were cut to pieces during the Second Battle of Manassas—have been seen beckoning by the woods at the western end of the park, clad in their red pantaloons, white leggings, and nightcap hats," wrote Diane McLellan in *Washingtonian* magazine in a characteristic description of what other witnesses have attested to. Variations on this story have involved a headless Zouave searching for his head, a lost companion, or possibly his way off the battlefield he marched onto so long before.

Stories concerning the Stone House, built in 1824 and run as an inn for drovers before the railroad largely supplanted them, are even more disturbing and gruesome. Used as a Confederate hospital during the Second Battle of Manassas, an account from a northern surgeon at the site states that Union troops were not just neglected but deliberately treated badly at the facility and that many of them died lingering or degrading deaths as a result.

"These inexperienced surgeons performed operations upon our men in a most horrible manner," testified Dr. J.M. Homiston of Brooklyn. "The young surgeons, who seemed to delight in hacking butchering [our men], were not, it would seem, permittde to perform any operations upon the rebel wounded."

With trauma like that associated with the place, it should not be surprising that so many reports of paranormal phenomena are associated with the Stone House, and written accounts from at least the early twentieth century claim that it is cursed in addition to anything else. It would seem that some sort of unquiet spirits occupy the place, and incidents people have reported include hearing footsteps in the unoccupied rooms above them and having glasses knocked off their faces.

I have only visited Manassas National Battlefield Park once, and that was relatively recently, in November 2006, with my daughter Hayley, grandma Val, and grandpa Jim. I will not say it is unfortunate that it has been unseasonably bright and sunny during my visits to a great many of the places described in this book. But, suffice it to say, such seemingly ideal conditions have certainly allowed me to assess the odds of various sites being haunted without atmospheric distractions like wind, rain, cold, darkness, or any number of other factors that could enhance the appearance that they are. And so, for a day near the end of the year, it was strikingly warm and clear during our trip to the battlefield.

After touring the exhibits in the Henry Hill Visitor Center and watching an orientation film titled "Manassas: End of Innocence," we decided to walk the one-mile loop trail that meanders across the rolling terrain corresponding to where the first battle was fought. During the walk we passed a number of interesting features, including a recreation of the Henry House, which had been blown up during the battle—along with the old woman living in it, who became the first civilian casualty of the war. We were also able to look northwest from a point on the trail to the Stone House, the most characteristic landmark at the park, which was used as a field hospital for soldiers of both sides during each of the battles. It was all very pleasant and informative (especially the revelation that the remains of the now-vanished village of Groveton lie within the park, a whole separate source of potential investigation for ghosthunters).

It was not until we reached the end of the trail, back again near the visitor center, that I spotted something that gave me some pause. It was a statue of Thomas "Stonewall" Jackson that had been erected in the 1930s and was in a style that I recognized but knew was not familiar to most Americans. In it, the mounted Jackson was almost ludicrously muscled, his chest outthrust in a heroic pose, his overall appearance suggesting Superman in a kepi and beard. He was, in fact, depicted in a style of art frequently characterized as "heroic realism" that is most commonly associated with the Nazi, Communist, and other totalitarian regimes of the 20th century. It had been erected, I suspected—considering the era when it had been dedicated—by people who, like Jackson himself, had attitudes toward civil war, race, and any number of other subjects completely alien to my own. It, more than anything else at the Manassas Battlefield, gave me a sense that the dead might yet have cause to walk the ground where they fought a century-and-a-half before, the issues for which they died still unresolved.

Statue of Stonewall Jackson

CHAPTER 5

Historic Occoquan
OCCOQUAN

There still are a number of old houses and buildings at Occoquan which have survived the damages of time and nature ... Also surviving, and quite active today, are a host of ghosts from Occoquan's past, so many, in fact, that it almost seems there is a haunt of one kind or another in just about every other building.

—L. B. Taylor Jr., "A Village Full of Spectral Visions"

DURING THE TIME WE HAVE LIVED in northern Virginia, my wife and I have visited Occoquan, an old and storied riverside village seven miles due south of our house, perhaps a half dozen times. It is surprisingly close for such a historic place, and always fun to walk around in and have a drink at, but is outside the sphere of our day-to-day activities, and years often go by between visits.

In the seventeen years that we have lived just up the road from the village, of course, we have driven past it hundreds of times on Ox Road, a historic thoroughfare that, from where we pick it up, runs north into Fairfax and south through Occoquan to an entry point onto I-95 that is convenient for trips to points south.

When my kids were young, I used to explain to them that the town was named for the schools of octopus that would migrate up through Chesapeake Bay and into inland waterways like the Occoquan River. As we would speed over the bridge that passes over both the river and the town, I would tell them to keep their eyes open for the octopuses frisking through the water below and leaping through it like eight-armed dolphins.

My youngest daughter, Hayley, was always a good sport about it all, and invariably claimed to see the tentacular beasts as they breached the water on their spirited romps. My oldest daughter, Lindsey, who might not have actually had a sense of humor when she was growing up, may never have truly looked to see if the creatures were there, preferring to indignantly insist that they could not be.

Ghost stories, presumably, would have not met with much more approval from Lindsey, and—if they were good enough— might very well have unnecessarily scared the hell out of Hayley. But there are ghost stories aplenty associated with Occoquan, and it would not be stretching the case much to say I might have been able to tell a different one every time we drove past the waterfront village.

"Occoquan" actually means "at the end of the water" in the language of the Doeg Indians, the aboriginal inhabitants of the area, who subsisted by fishing the local waters, hunting

for the ducks, geese, and other waterfowl, and by growing corn
and other vegetables in the fertile riparian soil. They were there
when the first English colonists explored the area and occupied
it until near the end of the 17th century, when they abruptly disappeared, probably as the result of epidemic disease, genocide,
or forced migration.

Settlers, fortunately, did not let the premium location
go to waste, and it soon grew into a significant commercial
and industrial community that made full use of its proximity to Chesapeake Bay. A warehouse for tobacco was built in
the 1730s, and the community grew steadily over the following decades. By the end of the century, Occoquan was home
to forges, water-driven grist mills, saw mills, cotton mills, bak-
eries, shipyards, and numerous storehouses, as well as dwellings of many sorts. One of its most significant industrial sites
was the Merchant's Mill, the first automated grist mill in the
country, which could be operated by a single man and used to
remove grain from ships and barges, process it into flour, and
return it to the vessels for transport to locations throughout the
Americas. It operated for 175 years, until it was destroyed in
1916 by a fire that ravaged the town.

That fire, along with silting in the river, ruined Occoquan
as an industrial and commercial district. It survived, however,
and today has an economy based largely on weekend tourism,
which it serves through numerous restaurants, galleries, boutiques, jewelry stores, and a marina. And many of the historic
buildings in which those businesses are located are reputed to
be haunted.

About midway on Mill Street, the main thoroughfare along
the river on which most of the town's restaurants and shops
are located, is the Occoquan Inn, which has one of the greatest
reputations for being haunted. It is a very old establishment,
and its middle section and brick fireplace are part of a residence

that was originally built in 1810 and which its owners opened up
to travelers, so that it gradually became known as an inn. Today,
it is a fine-dining restaurant, and is believed to be haunted by
the last of the Doeg Indians to dwell in the vicinity of the village. According to legend, an unnamed Indian had an inordi-
nate interest in the innkeeper's wife and one night snuck into
the inn with an eye toward visiting the object of his affection,
but was found out by the innkeeper, who shot him dead. Since
then, visitors have periodically reported seeing his likeness in
the smoke issuing forth from the building's chimney and at
various places within the inn, particularly in the upstairs ladies'
restroom, where he has startled a number of women who have
seen his face in the mirror.

My wife and I had our own odd experience at the Occoquan
Inn in September 2007, when we had dinner there to celebrate
our anniversary. Whether it was indicative of a ghostly presence
I am really not sure.

The restaurant was not crowded, with no more than two of
the other tables occupied at any given time, and we were sitting
at a corner table in one of the Inn's little dining areas, so we had a
good deal of privacy. Both the food and the service were good, and
we enjoyed our champagne and each other's company throughout
most of our meal without noticing anything out of the ordinary.

Toward the end of the meal, however, we heard something
that caught our attention, and almost simultaneously looked
up at the spot on the ceiling above us from which the sound
seemed to be coming. There, just beyond the intervening layer
of plaster, we could distinctly hear what sounded like the pitter-
patter of little feet, scratching, and other activities too obscure
to clearly identify.

At the time, we thought these sounds might indicate rodent
inhabitants of the inn, although we were by no means certain.

We didn't say anything to the restaurant staff, both because it enhanced our visit rather than detracted from it and because we did not want to unleash any sort of retribution against any little animal that might have been making its home in the inn. Upon reflection of the inn's haunted reputation, however, we had to reassess to some extent what we had heard and wonder if it might have indeed been something paranormal. I couldn't help but recall the classic H.P. Lovecraft horror story, "Dreams in the Witch House," in which a Colonial-era house is haunted by, among other things, the rat-like familiar of an ancient sorceress.

Numerous other buildings in Occoquan are reputed to be haunted as well.

The 18th-century house at 206 Mill Street, for example, which faces the river and the old town common, is currently occupied by a boutique, an acupuncturist, a massage therapist, and a life coach. It has long also been occupied by a ghost various residents have dubbed "Charlotte," who seems to become excited whenever new merchandise is brought into whatever store is at that time doing business in the building. On such days, she has sometimes been heard clattering noisily down the stairs, as if to get a look at the new items. She has also been known to have rearranged new inventory at night when the store is closed, presumably to display it in a manner more becoming to her own taste. And, perhaps even more mysteriously, she has been known to leave behind a single flower, which proprietors have found when they opened up the next morning.

At 302 Mill Street is the building built in the 1860s that was long known as Leary's Lumber and Hardware Store, and which supplied the town and the surrounding area with general merchandise. Old Mrs. Leary is reputed to have not liked noisy children much—but then who does?—and to have frequently chased them off and tried to keep the area around her store quiet. People

have reported seeing her, typically after the store is closed, standing behind the original sales counter that is still set up inside the
store's front window. Some claim to have seen her shaking her
finger at unruly passersby. Today, the corner store is occupied by
four different shops, among them two art galleries.

Since 1997, the old wood-frame building at 307 Mill Street
has been occupied by Brambles, a store that specializes in artsy
home and garden accessories. It has apparently been occupied
since long before that by a female ghost who has been spotted
by some people carrying a lighted candle. She has also been
known, especially during the winter, to leave a lighted candle
sitting on the counter during the night, which the store owners have found burning when they arrived to open up in the
morning.

Seven businesses are currently located in the building at
309 Mill Street, including an artists' cooperative, an art gallery,
a jewelry store, a number of engineering or construction firms,
and a law office. It was once a successful funeral parlor that
served the needs of a two-county area. Local legends say severe
flooding once smashed open the store front and washed out a
number of coffins—with or without bodies in them is somewhat unclear—and swept them downstream, which could certainly contribute to some ongoing spiritual agitation. At least
one ghost is believed to haunt the property, and some people
believe it is the former undertaker, clad in the formal dark frock
coat of his trade, looking back in on his former establishment.
Among other things, people have reported hearing footsteps in
parts of the building when it is empty of living occupants.

Seven shops also occupy the building at 313 Mill Street,
near its far end, including Miller's Lighthouse, which has been
located there for more than thirty years. It was built around
1888 with bricks brought over from England that were used as
ballast in ships that made port at Occoquan. From around the

turn of the 19th century, its lower level was used as a general store, and upper areas served as a home for the owner and his family. No one seems to know the name of the ghost that currently occupies the site, but store owners have reported hearing strange whispered voices; finding display cases standing open when they should have been locked; and having merchandise moved around—and, in a few instances, even thrown across the room in the presence of customers! Business owners have also reported finding sooty footprints in a part of the building that had contained a coal bunker when it was built.

Constructed around 1760, the building at 406 Mill Street is believed to be the oldest extant home in Occoquan, and currently houses a hair stylist. Not much is known about the female ghost occupying the building, but she has been seen a number of times over the years (although her coiffure is likely outdated, and perhaps she is only seeking a new look).

MOVING A BLOCK INLAND from Mill Street up to 201 Union Street brings one to "The Courtyard," an L-shaped building constructed with bricks baked at a kiln on the other side of the river (the remains of which still exist at Occoquan Park). It was the site of the town well, and today houses five businesses, including a candy shop and an ice cream store. It is not known whether or not the resident ghost has a sweet tooth, but it seems certain that he likes his quiet, because the owners always find their wind chimes mysteriously torn down.

A block down Poplar Alley at 204 Washington Street is a wood-framed building constructed in 1910 that currently houses an antique shop. It is reputed to harbor several ghosts, some of which have even been seen during the day, according to various witnesses.

Beyond the publicly accessible places in Occoquan, there are also a great many historical private homes that have long had a reputation for being haunted. There are so many, in fact, and Occoquan is such a small town—about one-fifth of a square mile in area with a living population of only about eight hundred— that one has to wonder if it might not have one of the highest haunting indices in the state. The inhabitants of the town seem to have established a good working relationship with their ghostly cohabitants, however, and to consider them one of the many elements that give the little waterfront village its charm.

CHAPTER 6

Rippon Lodge
WOODBRIDGE

Many tragic stories are told of Rippon Lodge. More than one murder is said to have been committed there. A victim of a fatal duel bled to death on the parlor floor. This house is said to be haunted in such a ghostly and sinister fashion that no one will occupy it, and the public road has changed its course to avoid the neighborhood.

—Manassas Journal, May 19, 1911

WHILE IT HAD A PRESENCE ominous enough to be commented on in newspapers a century ago, Rippon Lodge has since become somewhat more obscure, if not actually less menacing. Although I had read about it in Marguerite DuPont Lee's excellent and florid *Virginia Ghosts* (and lived only fourteen miles from it for seventeen years), I was not even sure it still existed until the day I visited it for the first time in June 2008.

Rippon Lodge is today, in fact, believed to be the oldest house extant in Prince William County. Built in the 1720s by planter Richard Blackburn, it sits on a hillside overlooking Neabsco Creek, the waters of which flow into the nearby Potomac River. Its prosperous owner built his home along the King's Highway— roughly corresponding to modern-day Route 1—a critical roadway that stretched from Newport, Rhode Island, to Yorktown, Virginia, and connected the original thirteen colonies (and played a critical role in the Revolutionary War, being used as the route taken by the American troops who defeated the British at Yorktown). Blackburn named it for Ripon, in North Yorkshire, England, the city where he was born (variant spellings being much more prevalent in the 18th century than they are today). According to some sources, it is referred to as a lodge because it was also used as a Masonic meeting place.

Established as the seat of a cotton and tobacco plantation, the somewhat modest home overlooked about 21,000 acres of land and, despite its proximity to the colonial seaport town of Dumfries, had its own port on Neabsco Creek. Clustered about the wooded ridgeline above the house are the ancient graves of some of its earliest inhabitants, many of them now marked only with worn and illegible stones or grassy mounds, including those of Blackburn and some of his family's slaves.

Blackburn bequeathed the property to his son, Colonel Thomas Blackburn, who had less allegiance to the home country than his father and during the Revolutionary War served as an aide to George Washington, who was himself a frequent guest at the estate. Another visitor to the lodge during this era was militia Captain Bernard J. Hooe, who in April 1810 fought

Rippon Lodge was a modest home overlooking 21,000 acres.

a duel with James Kemp just across the Potomac in Maryland. Hooe was critically injured in the fight and brought back across the river to Rippon Lodge, where he died soon after.

By the time Blackburn and his wife followed Hooe into the great beyond, Rippon Lodge had acquired the beginnings of its dark reputation and remained vacant for some years, apparently never passing on to anyone else in their family.

It was eventually purchased around 1820 by new owners, the Atkinsons, who owned it for about a century. The first suggestions that it was haunted were made during the era they lived in the house, and over the years members of the Atkinson family described various ghostly phenomena, including "strange and disturbing noises."

Rippon Lodge was not sold to new owners until 1924, when Wade Ellis, a Federal judge from Washington, D.C., purchased it, and subsequently made significant efforts to preserve and renovate it. Interestingly, some time after taking possession of it, Ellis discovered that he was a descendant of Richard Blackburn, the man who had built the home (although it is not clear at what point he discovered this and to what extent it influenced his preservation efforts).

Ellis eventually sold Rippon Lodge to another Blackburn descendant, Rear Admiral Richard Blackburn Black, who accompanied Rear Admiral Richard E. Byrd on his Antarctic explorations. Black's daughter inherited the house from him in 1989, and eleven years later sold it to Prince William County, which now maintains it and the surrounding forty acres of property.

One of the most often-told ghost stories associated with Rippon Lodge has its roots in the era of Thomas Blackburn, who married a daughter of an ill-tempered family known locally as the "Rattlesnake" Grahams. She was apparently as irascible as the rest of her clan, and is said to have one day impatiently knocked out of her way the young child of a house slave, whose head struck the stone jamb of a fireplace. The child died from her injury, casting a pall over the house and leaving her mother inconsolable. Mistress Blackburn was indifferent to what in no way would have at that time been considered a crime (there is some suggestion that she might have eventually been somewhat remorseful but, no reason being given for this change of heart, this is likely merely the opinion of latter-day apologists).

Some people have claimed to see a bloody stain at the spot where the child's head was ruptured on the stone of the fireplace, and others believe that her spirit hovers over the spot where she was buried on the hill above. This callous and unjust killing bestowed a curse on the house and made it prone to possession by subsequent spirits. Many of the phenomena that have been reported over the years do not have the hallmarks typical of a child ghost.

One of the most dramatic early episodes involved a pair of friends from Alexandria on a hiking trip who decided to take shelter in the abandoned house in the years before it was purchased by the Atkinsons. Soon after they turned in for the night, they began to hear loud and continuous noises, which eventually gave way to shrieks and peals of ghoulish laughter. Alarmed by this eerie clamor, the young men produced a light and proceeded to search the place from top to bottom to determine the source. They were unnerved to discover that it was deserted and, darkness notwithstanding, abandoned it immediately. Relating their experience to people in the surrounding neighborhood the next morning, they learned the name of the house and that it was widely known throughout the local area to be haunted.

My friend Jason Froehlich and I did not, fortunately, experience anything quite so dramatic during our brief visit to Rippon Lodge (but, of course, we did not try to spend the night there). We learned of its continued existence while chatting with Beth Cardinale, administrator of the haunted Weems-Botts Museum, located about four-and-a-half miles away, and decided to take advantage of its proximity and visit it that same day.

Unfortunately, the first thing we learned is that it is open only on Friday, Saturday, and Sunday, and not Tuesday (which was the day we visited), our first clue being that the gate blocking the main road leading up to the house was closed. We turned around, headed back down Blackburn Road toward Route 1, and almost immediately came to a turnoff that was marked as a staff entrance to the site (someone was close on our tail as we made a hasty turn onto this road; thus we did not notice until we left the admonitions against anyone else using this alternate approach).

We crawled up the narrow, wooded, and badly rutted dirt road for a few hundred yards, after which we passed a private home and then right afterward emerged onto the open area in front of Rippon Lodge. We stopped the car and got out to get a better look at the ancient house, which appeared to be beautifully restored and very well maintained. A number of other structures were clustered around the site, including a small cabin to our right, a covered well at one side of the front lawn, and another building behind the lodge itself.

It was very quiet around Rippon Lodge, and no one else seemed to be there but us, giving the place a somewhat desolate air. Despite the brightness of the day and the evidence of use, if not actual occupation, a gloomy aura seemed to hang over the otherwise pleasant-looking old building. Whether it was this oppressive atmosphere—or merely the growing sense that we were not meant to be there at that time—we started to feel disquieted and nervous and decided not to linger any longer than necessary.

The road appeared to go completely around the lodge and loop back on itself, so we decided that following it back to where we started would be easier than trying to turn around, and that we might as well see the other side of it before we left. Driving toward the house and then circling around it, we stopped several times on our circumnavigation of the lodge to take pictures and get a closer look at various details. I kept an eye on the windows and doors of the structure as we went, looking for any signs that the building might be occupied by either living people or spirits, but did not detect signs of either.

Coming back around toward the front of the lodge and facing back in the direction from which we had come, we could look down the hillside and see through a break in the trees the waters of the Potomac River, and it was obvious to us why someone would have wanted to build here. Maybe a spot that is breathtaking and beautiful enough, I thought, could induce someone to linger at it long after their spirit should have moved on to another world.

Whatever might have allowed any of the former inhabitants of Rippon Lodge to remain there after the normal termination of their lives, the mysteries and legends of the place have carried over through the course of three centuries. And, after even a brief sojourn at the antiquated house, we could readily sense why this would have been the case.

CHAPTER 7

Weems-Botts Museum
DUMFRIES

She could not remember ever being truly happy in her adult life; her years with her mother had been built up devotedly around small guilts and small reproaches, constant weariness, and unending despair .... Caring for her mother, lifting a cross old lady from her chair to her bed, setting out endless little trays of soup and oatmeal, steeling herself to the filthy laundry.

—Shirley Jackson, *The Haunting of Hill House*

MUCH OF WHAT MANY OF US LEARNED about George Washington while we were growing up—including

bizarre legends of him chopping down cherry trees apropos of
nothing but truthfully confessing to his actions—were concocted
by a man named Mason Locke Weems, a parson who dwelled in
Dumfries, Virginia, in the early years of the American republic.
His bookstore is one of three Colonial-era buildings extant in
the little town, and is today the only one open to the public and
known as the Weems-Botts Museum, being named for him and
a subsequent owner, lawyer Benjamin Botts.

Today, the Weems-Botts property is believed by many of
the people who have visited or worked at it over the years to be
haunted, and a great number of inexplicable and paranormal
phenomena has been associated with it.

"There have been things that have happened here that I
can't explain, for which there is no logical explanation," Beth
Cardinale, administrator of the Weems-Botts Museum, told me
when I visited it with my friend Jason Froehlich the last Tuesday
in June 2008.

Dumfries is a very old town, of course—the oldest continuously chartered town in Virginia, as a matter of fact—and places
like it tend to have the greatest incidence of ghostly phenomena.
It is located on land that was first explored by John Smith in 1608,
and was inhabited at that time by the Doeg Indians, a tribe of
hunters, fishers, farmers, miners, and traders. The first European
settlement of the site appears to have been in 1690, when someone built a grist mill on the banks of nearby Quantico Creek.

The fledgling community did not grow much for a number
of years, until a customs house and warehouse were built in
1731, the year the county was formed, followed by a number of
additional warehouses the next year. At the prompting of the
Scottish merchants who operated out of it, Dumfries was chartered in 1749 as the first town in Prince William County, and
named for the hometown in Scotland of the man who owned the
land on which it was established. Three years later, the Quantico

Episcopal Church was built, the first in the county, with bricks
brought over from England.

Dumfries grew up at the juncture of two major roads, the
north-south King's Highway (known before that as the Potomac
Path locally and today as Route 1) and the east-west Duke Street,
which linked the town with Winchester to the west (and is now
also known as Route 234).

While it is a sleepy, little-known town today, Dumfries was
a vital commercial center during the Colonial era—indeed, the
second most important port in Colonial America at one point—
and the volume of goods shipped from it was comparable to that
moved through Boston, New York, or Philadelphia. Ships bound
to or from England, Scotland, Holland, France, and the West
Indies sailed into Dumfries with manufactured goods and out of
it with tobacco, wheat, and lumber. One of the largest shipments
of tobacco to leave from the colonies was shipped from Dumfries,
which was the center of all trade in northern Virginia.

Amenities in the prosperous town—many housed in buildings of significant architectural value—included a variety of
stores, numerous private and public warehouses, several hotels,
a dance hall, an opera house, a jockey club, a race track, a newspaper, a bank, a silversmith, a brick factory, multiple academies,
a cabinetmaker, a clockmaker, and a blacksmith. At its peak,
during the period 1760 to 1822, when it also served as the third
seat of the county, Dumfries had a population of two thousand
and was an important center of commercial and social interaction. During its heyday, luminaries like George Washington
were frequent visitors to the town, and it was home to many of
the first families of the region, among them the Lees, Grahams,
Graysons, Hendersons, and Tebbs.

Eventually, Dumfries' harbor silted up, and that, coupled
with primitive farming methods that ruined much of the rich
surrounding farmlands, wrecked the economy of the town and

brought its prosperity to an end. Today, it is little more than a village and suburb of Washington, D.C.

It was during its golden age, in 1798, that Parson Mason Locke Weems purchased the oldest portion of the property that is now the Weems-Botts Museum—which had originally been constructed around 1750 at the corner of Duke and Cameron Streets as the vestry house for the Quantico Episcopal Church—and used it as a bookstore and warehouse. Two years later, he wrote his famous work of mythology on Washington, becoming his first biographer and greatest apologist, and followed it with works on Francis Marion, Benjamin Franklin, and William Penn. A true Renaissance man, Weems was educated as a minister and doctor and was also a merchant and talented musician.

Weems sold the house just four years after he acquired it, in 1802, to lawyer Benjamin Botts, a young go-getter who used it as his law office until his untimely death in 1811, in a theater fire in Richmond. Botts achieved some measure of fame when Aaron Burr, Thomas Jefferson's vice president, requested that he serve as the youngest member of his defense team during his trial for treason.

While the Weems-Botts house is apparently haunted by the ghosts of two former inhabitants, it seems that neither of those two are believed to be the men for which the property is named, both of whom appear to have passed on to the afterlife uneventfully (or, at the least, gone on to haunt other places). It may seem surprising that neither of them should be among those suspected of haunting the house, but a little investigation and reflection explains why.

First, neither of them actually died within the house or even owned it very long, which would have limited their emotional or spiritual attachments to it.

Second, neither appears to have left behind unfinished business or to have been tormented by an unfulfilled life. Weems in particular seems to have been very satisfied with himself, and to have successfully and zealously devoted the greater part of his intellectual, emotional, and spiritual life to his deity (who, by all accounts, was Washington, "the HERO and the Demigod," who he characterizes as "Jupiter Conservator" or "Jupiter the Savior").

No, two far more tragic and unfulfilled lives are associated with the house and seem to be the source of the unhappy spirits who continue to dwell within it. And, as Beth Cardinale was to explain to us, their names are Mamie and Violet, a pair of sisters who lived in the house during the last century. Their stories are as strange and gothic as any I have found associated with a purportedly haunted site.

In 1869, four years after the Civil War ended, Richard Merchant purchased the Weems-Botts house and for the next century his family lived in it. Whether he was married to his wife Annie at that time, who then would have been about thirteen, is unclear.

Richard and Annie Merchant's first daughter, Mamie, was born around 1883. She suffered from some sort of epilepsy and, with the hardened propriety of that era, the family kept her confined within an upstairs bedroom to hide her condition from the public. She was never allowed to leave the room, taking her meals at a small table and even performing hygiene functions within the room's confines. It is not surprising that her intellectual development was supposed to have been stunted, and that she was to remain childlike her entire life—which was not long, as she succumbed to a seizure in 1906, at the age of twenty-three.

Violet's life was to be more prolonged but, in its way, equally grim. She was apparently blessed with good health, both physically and mentally. She lived away from home somewhere outside of Dumfries, had a job, and a fiancé. When her father, Richard, died a few months before Mamie, her mother demanded that she return home and take care of her. Dutifully, she left behind her husband-to-be, her job, her life, and returned to the family home in Dumfries (presumably in time to be present for Mamie's convulsive demise).

There is some suggestion that Violet thought her mother might not live long and that she might be able to return to the existence she had enjoyed elsewhere, but that hope waned, slowly but surely, one long, lonely year after another, until nearly half a century had passed. Annie hung on until 1954, when she died at age ninety-eight. Violet herself lived on just another thirteen years, many of them in a nursing home, and died in 1967. (Violet's life could almost have been the inspiration for Eleanor in Shirley Jackson's 1959 novel *The Haunting of Hill House*—adapted for the screen in 1963 and 1999 as *The Haunting*—the main difference being that the literary character cared for her mother just eleven years.)

A few years after Violet died, the city of Dumfries acquired the house and, in cooperation with the Historic Dumfries nonprofit association, has operated it as a museum since 1976. It was around the time they were renovating it for this public use that ghostly phenomena were first recorded at the house.

Beth showed me and Jason around the Weems-Botts house during our visit and told us about some of the strange experiences she has had at the house. She had her first, in fact, during one of her initial visits to it several years ago, at one of the sleepovers the institution allows each year in October.

"Throughout the night I would wake up occasionally, because I heard creaking, groaning, old house noises, pipe-rattling noises," she said. "I've been in old houses; I've heard the plumbing rattle, so it was not an unfamiliar sound." She was sleeping in what is called the "Weems Room," she said, and most of the noise was coming from the nearby parlor.

"The next day, the curator asked me how I'd slept," she said. When Beth described to the woman what had disturbed her sleep throughout the night, "she smiled and said to me, 'There's no plumbing in this house!'"

Beth went on to describe another incident, which occurred during a visit by a group of high-school students after Beth had begun working at the house. They were in the upstairs bedroom used by Violet, which is in the oldest part of the house, and has a window that used to look out onto an open area prior to the building being expanded but now faces only a brick wall. She and one of the students were talking in the room and the window, just a few feet away from them, was closed.

"I turned to point to the window to explain something and it was open," she said. "We both kind of looked at it, and I said, 'Oh, that's just our ghost saying "hello,"' and he chuckled. I talked some more to him, and when we looked back at the window it was closed again." None of the other windows were open and there was no breeze and no one else had been present.

"The next day, I was in the room with two young ladies, and asked if they knew about the ghost." They did not, and seemed to be a little taken aback by this information. "'We didn't know anything about a ghost!' they said. I told them not to worry and that nothing usually happened there. All of a sudden, the window rattled, and the girls started heading for the steps!"

Another story predated Beth by about a decade, and had been related to her by people who worked at Weems-Botts at the time. It involved an officer from nearby Marine Corps Base Quantico, who was there with a group of Boy Scouts touring the house. They were in the other upstairs bedroom, the one in which Mamie had been confined, and the docent was speaking to the group. Turning to the Marine scout leader, she could see that he was visibly shaken and looking toward the far corner of the room.

"She needs her chair," he said in a quavering voice, sweat breaking out on his forehead, and then abruptly rushed from the house. He could not be induced for any reason to return to it, and the museum guide had to gather up the scouts and lead them out herself.

Other stories Beth told us involved minor but strange episodes involving various artifacts displayed throughout the house. In a parlor, for example, a doll that had belonged to Violet is normally left sitting on one of the chairs. And there it would be when the staff locked up at night, but when they returned in the morning, the doll would be elsewhere in the room. This continued until one of the docents made a firm declaration that whoever kept moving the doll should stop—after which they did. Yet another episode in recent memory involved a mislabeled photograph that would not stay on the wall until the proper name was affixed to it.

A very recent episode occurred just a few days before our visit. A woman had come by the museum to talk to Beth and had gone to the Weems-Botts house, rather than the annex where the administrative offices are located. When she finally made it to the right place, she told Beth she had seen a woman looking out of an upstairs window—the window to Mamie's room—but had been unable to get into the locked building or induce the woman to come down and let her in. Somewhat disquieted by this, Beth verified that none of her people had been in the building at all that day, and that whoever the visitor had seen had not been one of them.

Beth told us several more stories about strange occurrences at the museum during the following hour that we spent with her, both firsthand and as recounted to her by others. There seemed to be little doubt in her mind that it was, indeed, thoroughly haunted.

Neither Jason nor I experienced any sort of overt paranormal phenomena during our visit to Weems-Botts, but the atmosphere in Mamie's little room started to grow oppressive during the fifteen minutes or so we spent in it, despite its neat, bright appearance. It was easy to see how someone with severe health issues would not have been improved by a lifetime of confinement in it, and how a spirit deranged by such seclusion might have become

Strange events that occurred at the Weems-Botts Museum include a doll being moved from the chair where it is normally kept and tags attached to and hidden under some irons being pulled out and left hanging.

trapped within it, unable to escape in death the prison that it had occupied in life. So, too, was it all too easy to understand how Violet, deprived of a normal existence and trapped by bonds as solid as any walls, might be dismally continuing her grim vigil.

Something unseen certainly seems to be dwelling at Weems-Botts, and it seems likely that it is the women who spent within it their unhappy lives. Whether they are trying to establish in death the relationships they were deprived of in life or instead reacting to the unfamiliar intrusion of strangers into their solitude is yet a mystery.

CENTRAL

VIRGINIA: CENTRAL AREA

North Carolina

Danville
  Wreck of the Old 97

Gordonsville
  Civil War Museum at the Exchange Hotel

Petersburg
  Trapezium House

Pittsylvania County
  Berry Hill Road

Richmond
  Poe Museum

CHAPTER 8

Berry Hill Road
PITTSYLVANIA COUNTY

Certain it is, the place still continues under the sway of some witching power ... The whole neighborhood abounds with local tales, haunted spots, and twilight superstitions; stars shoot and meteors glare oftener across the valley than in any other part of the country.

—Washington Irving, "The Legend of Sleepy Hollow"

BERRY HILL ROAD AND THE AREA through which
it wends are creepy under the best of circumstances, and it is
easy to see how someone visiting them in darkness might con-
clude they are haunted. In addition, the stretch of country road
and the rural thoroughfares branching off it are also home to a
number of other reputed paranormal phenomena.

This road does, in fact, have a widespread reputation for
weirdness in the Danville area, as my wife, Diane, and I discovered while ghosthunting there the week between Christmas
and New Year in 2007. We had gone in search of ghosts associated with the wreck of the Old 97, a train that had derailed in
1903, but nearly everyone we talked to dismissed it and directed
us instead to Berry Hill Road.

It was an unseasonably bright, sunny, and warm afternoon
as my wife and I headed east on Riverside Drive out of Danville,
following the directions we had been given by various people.
We had, in fact, spent part of the previous evening drinking
martinis with Colie Walker, night manager for the restaurant at
the hotel where we had stayed the night, and he had given us an
earful about the place. His stories included accounts of ghostly
little girls jumping rope near the willow tree under which their
bodies were buried; a span dubbed "Satan's Bridge" where the
spectral form of a young man who supposedly hanged himself
there has reportedly been seen; a stretch of highway in front of
a witch's house on which cars will roll uphill rather than down;
and the slaughtered carcasses of animals hung from trees. It is
also reputedly an active stomping ground for the Ku Klux Klan.
In short, Sleepy Hollow, Southern style.

Just a few miles past the line for Pittsylvania County, we
came to the intersection with Berry Hill Road and turned left.
From where it begins at Riverside Drive, Berry Hill Road twists
about seven-and-a-half-miles, generally heading southwest, until
reaching the North Carolina state line, where its name changes

to T. Clarence Stone Highway. In its relatively short stretch through Virginia, however, the road has a markedly distinct character, which became obvious to us almost immediately.

Near its start, a number of other roads lead off in either direction from Berry Hill Road: those to the north generally past older, modest, relatively small houses, and those to the south past larger, more affluent homes and farms. Soon after passing these, however, the road begins to run through dense woodland punctuated by miles-long stretches of devastated-looking blight, mostly on the south side of the road. Periodically, tucked back in the wood line, we could see abandoned, vegetation-choked farmsteads and rutted dirt roads (that probably don't appear on any maps) twist away into the forest. Many were blocked by makeshift gates emblazoned with signs warning visitors away. To say that the area felt ominous and unwelcoming would be an understatement.

At the intersection with Oak Hill Road, we went north for awhile, and eventually came to a small country church, the first thing we had seen in several miles. We decided not to go any further at that point, and turned around. Approaching the intersection with Berry Hill Road again, we noticed at the side of the road the mangled carcass of a large animal, possibly a deer, with its exposed and bloody ribcage turned skyward.

We continued on Berry Hill Road, and soon after saw, at the left side of the road, a large rock painted with a white cross. Overhead, both in the air and perched on nearby utility poles and trees, an uncannily large number of vultures watched over the place and regarded us as we passed.

At the intersection with Stateline Bridge Road, just past a set of railroad tracks, we went south. We turned past a pickup truck stopped at the three-way stop that was turning onto Berry Hill Road, and I noticed the driver, a white guy with a mustache and baseball cap. As we moved down the road, I saw him make a U-turn and begin to follow us.

Rock with cross by the side of Berry Hill Road

As we sped down the road, the creep in the pickup stayed behind us, and after about a mile we broke out of the wood line onto a low concrete span over a river. As we reached the other side of it, we passed a sign welcoming us to North Carolina, and the name of the road changed to Berry Hill Bridge Road. We went about another mile, until we reached an intersection near a farm where we could turn around, and as we did the pickup truck passed us and continued on its way.

Returning to the bridge from the other direction, I was stunned to see that it was completely covered with graffiti, something that while driving into the sun and keeping an eye on my rear-view mirror I had not noticed previously. Colie Walker had described "Satan's Bridge" as being tagged (an urbanized term for "painted" that, when I explained it to my wife, both baffled and annoyed her). Its location corresponded exactly with the directions Walker had given us, and so it seemed we had found the cursed bridge.

Driving back across to the Virginia side, we went a few hundred yards to a spot where the road widened adequately for me to safely turn off and start to get my equipment ready for a walk back to the bridge. "I'm just going to wait in the car," my wife said as I started to get out of the vehicle, repeating a mantra that for her was as automatic and unanalyzed as "bless you" would have been in response to a sneeze. The creep with the pickup was on the other side of the river and I would see if he was coming back, so I didn't argue with her.

Heading toward the bridge along the left side of the road, I could see that the nearby woods were choked and tangled with heavy vine growth and had an almost quintessentially haunted look. I also had a growing sense of unease, and as I came nearer to the bridge I became increasingly aware of a sound like a howling wind, somewhere in the distance, that became more and more audible as I neared the span.

Walking out onto the sunlit bridge, I could hear a low, shrieking noise somewhere in the distance, like a wind ripping through the woods around me. Glancing at the wood line on either side of the river, I could see that it was perfectly still and could not feel so much as a light breeze. It sent a chill up my spine. It would have scared the hell out of me and made me feel like I was standing on the threshold to the netherworld if I'd been there at night, possibly alone, or under the influence.

I quickly walked to the far end of the bridge and, with the light at my back, got some photos. Most of the graffiti I passed seemed to be of the "X loves Y" and "Class of Z" variety, but there were a few pentagrams and devilish epithets mixed in with it. I also saw burnt-down candle stubs lying among the detritus of broken beer bottles on either side of the bridge. No one passed by during my time there, and I was completely alone as I looked down into the swirling ochre water of the Dan River and contemplated where the young man would have hanged himself if such an incident really had occurred here. The low, concrete bridge didn't look like it would be very convenient for that purpose—and his dangling specter would not have been visible by anyone on or at either end of it—and I wondered if he might not have used one of the trees in the surrounding vine-choked forest. It would have been, in any event, a morose and dismal place to die.

My need and desire to stay at the bridge sated, I trotted back toward the car and we resumed our exploration of the area.

Turning back onto Berry Hill Road and continuing south-west on it, we soon reached the point where it crossed the North Carolina state line. Almost immediately afterward, we heard a shrieking exactly like that of a jet engine, pulled over to the side of the road, and looked up, expecting to see an aircraft passing overhead and the noise to fade. There was nothing above us, however, and the noise remained steady for awhile longer before fading away.

We could see that the land across the road was fenced off and make out a small cluster of pipes and utility infrastructure. While we could not see anything that could have been making the great noise we heard, and while no signs offered an explanation for them or the fenced-off area from which they emanated, it seemed pretty obvious that we had stumbled onto some sort of industrial test facility—and that it had accounted for the distant noises I had heard at Satan's Bridge (a later perusal of maps and satellite imagery, however, did not reveal anything of that nature in that particular area). This new mystery being far beyond our purview, and with the sinister aspect of the neighborhood start-ing to weigh on us, we decided to leave it unexamined.

Heading back up Berry Hill Road toward where we had started, we made a few more exploratory stops before reaching the highway. We never did see the willow tree Walker had told us about, and we weren't sure of the exact location to try putting our car in neutral to see whether it would roll uphill. We saw so many dilapidated antebellum houses that we could not be certain which one was reputed to be the lair of the witch. But a couple of hours on Berry Hill Road were enough to convince us that there is probably a good reason for its reputation in the local area—and that we did not want to be lingering on it after dark.

CHAPTER 9

Exchange Hotel Civil War Hospital Museum
GORDONSVILLE

Bearing the bandages, water and sponge,
Straight and swift to my wounded I go,
Where they lie on the ground after the battle brought in,
Where their priceless blood reddens the grass the ground,
Or to the rows of the hospital tent, or under the roof'd hospital,
To the long rows of cots up and down each side I return,
To each and all one after another I drawn near, not one do
    I miss,
An attendant follows holding a tray, he carries a refuse pail,
Soon to be fill'd with clotted rags and blood, emptied, and
    fill'd again.

—Walt Whitman, "The Wound Dresser"

TO SAY THERE IS SOMETHING STRANGE going on at the Exchange Hotel Civil War Hospital Museum in Gordonsville would be somewhat of an understatement. My interaction with museum staff when I visited the site in May 2008 with my father, mother, and wife, left me inclined to believe that there was a reasonable chance the site was, indeed, haunted. But when I heard the irregular, garbled sounds that obscured my one-hour taped interview with curator Robert Kocovsky, I joined the ranks of definite believers.

This did not make me in any way unique, of course. The Exchange Hotel has for some time run ghost tours of the property for those with a casual interest in the subject, and has made provisions for ghosthunters and others with a stronger interest to conduct investigations overnight in the building. From what I understand, they are rarely disappointed.

A new era began for Gordonsville on January 1, 1840, when it became a stop on the Louisa Railroad—renamed the Virginia Central ten years later—allowing passengers to travel to and from the town and goods to be shipped from the farms and plantations of the surrounding area. Its first depot was opened in 1854, at the south end of Main Street, when the Orange and Alexandria Railroad extended its tracks from Orange to Gordonsville to connect with the existing line (a second depot was built in 1870 and its last one in 1904).

People coming into or departing from the depot frequented the nearby tavern run by Richard F. Omohundro, who did a brisk business in food and drink. When this establishment was razed by fire in 1859, Omohundro immediately built a beautiful new hotel, complete with high-ceilinged parlors and a grand veranda, on its ashes.

The elegant, three-story Exchange Hotel combined elements of Georgian architecture in the main section of the brick building, and Italianate architecture in its exterior features, both styles popular in the pre-war years. Other features included a restaurant on its lower level, spacious public rooms, a central hall with a wide staircase and handsome balustrade, and central halls running through each of the upper floors. It quickly became a popular and inviting spot for travelers.

When the Civil War began in 1861, towns like Gordonsville and the railroads that ran through them became critical strategic assets to the Confederate government. Railroads had never been used in warfare before but were to play a large role in the conflict that would eventually become referred to as "the first railroad war."

In March 1862, the Confederate military authorities took over the Exchange Hotel and established it as the headquarters of the Gordonsville Receiving Hospital, which provided medical care to tens of thousands of Northern and Southern troops over the following four years. Wounded soldiers from battlefields that included Brandy Station, Cedar Mountain, Chancellorsville, Mine Run, Trevilian Station, and the Wilderness were brought into town by rail, unloaded, and moved directly into the sprawling hospital compound that grew up around the former hotel.

In an era when men died of injury and disease in droves—about twice as many as those slain in combat—the Gordonsville Receiving Hospital was the exception to the rule, with a markedly lower death rate compared to most other contemporary medical facilities. Of the approximately 70,000 men treated at the hospital, only somewhat more than 700 died at the site, a much smaller proportion than what was typical for the conflict. The deceased were buried on the hospital grounds initially and then later exhumed and moved to the nearby Maplewood Cemetery. (According to Kocovsky, the spirits of some of the buried soldiers apparently remained behind, and the area where the cemetery was located has been the site of ghostly phenomena.)

Director of the hospital was Dr. B.M Lebby, who oversaw its operations through October 1865. Although pro-Confederate and a native of South Carolina, Lebby had received his medical training in the North and was both compassionate and proficient. The relatively low death rate at the hospital (a mere 26 Union soldiers) can be attributed to his humanity and skill as a physician and administrator.

After the war, the site served newly freed slaves as a Freedman's Bureau Hospital for several years before eventually reverting to use once again as a hotel. In 1971, Historic Gordonsville Inc., acquired the property, restored it, and converted it into a Civil War medical museum.

Today, the Civil War Museum at the Exchange Hotel contains exhibits on the history of Gordonsville, the hotel, and its transformation into a receiving hospital, the only one still standing in Virginia. It includes an impressive collection of artifacts relating to medical care during the war, including surgical instruments;

Exhibits at the Exchange Hotel Civil War Hospital Museum include rooms with original hospital furnishings and artifacts arranged as they would have likely appeared during the Civil War.

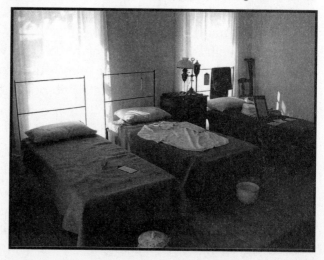

pharmaceutical bottles and containers; medical knapsacks and panniers; stretchers and litters; prosthetic devices; and even dental tools.

It is also home, Kocovsky said, to at least eleven ghosts that he and the staff have identified! The museum makes no secret of this presence, and touts it both in its published materials and highly popular ghost tours.

"It isn't necessary for our guides to purposefully frighten you as our 'permanent residents' often make their presence known," the tour description reads. "There have been numerous reports of apparitions as well as the many unexplained sounds described by past visitors."

While not all the ghosts have been identified by name or connected with specific historical figures known to have been associated with the Exchange Hotel, quite a few have, in part through the help of ghosthunters and psychic researchers who have visited the site.

A marker outside the museum alludes to the fact that the hospital tended to wounded soldiers of both the Northern and Southern armies during the Civil War.

One such ghost is Annie Smith, a black woman and the hotel's former cook, who has been spotted numerous times in the windows of and around the outbuilding used as a summer kitchen where she worked. Another is Mrs. Leevy, the wife of one of the doctors assigned to the hospital, who went mad during her stay at the site. And yet another is the aptly named George Plant, the facility's gravedigger, who has been known to waken reenactors camping out on the grounds surrounding the hotel. A number of nameless ghosts, believed to be those of Civil War soldiers who died at the hospital, quite possibly in agonizing surgical procedures or of one of the diseases that claimed so many lives, are also among those that haunt the site.

Kocovsky also told me about a dark, shadowy, and hostile ghost—whose name is yet unknown—who has frightened a number of people over the years, including, on one occasion, some police officers who were checking to make sure the building was properly locked up.

Other ghostly incidents people have reported at the museum include sightings of a spectral woman sitting as if upon a chair, even though one was not there, and photographs that have picked up a number of anomalies, including spirit orbs.

Despite the vast number of incidents that have occurred at the Civil War Museum at the Exchange Hotel, it is, unfortunately, a bit much to expect that one should experience anything similar during any particular visit (especially a first one, it would seem). Indeed, the museum itself echoes this sentiment in its materials: "As it is impossible to predict when these 'permanent residents' will make their presence known, we urge you to visit often."

Good advice indeed. Because if the strange, incomprehensible sounds—voices?—on the tape I walked away with is any indication, then the museum is well worth further investigation.

CHAPTER 10

Edgar Allan Poe Museum
RICHMOND

Thou wast that all to me, love
For which my soul did pine—
A green isle in the sea, love,
A fountain and a shrine,
All wreathed in fruit and flowers
And all the flowers were mine ...

        —Edgar Allan Poe, "To One in Paradise"

THERE IS NO DOUBT that the spirit of Edgar Allan Poe
lives on at the museum dedicated to him in Richmond. Whether
that spirit is attended by one or more ghosts, however, is an open
question.

When I met with Chris Semtner, a somewhat subdued artist in his early thirties who has served as curator for the Edgar
Allan Poe Museum for the past eight years, he was quick to state
that it is not haunted. During the hour or so my mother and I
spent chatting with him at the museum on a bright, sunny day
in early March 2008, however, he recounted episode after episode of incidents associated with the museum—many of them
firsthand—that most believers would accept as clear evidence of
ghostly presences.

Semtner does, in fact, believe that some places are haunted
and claims to have lived in one that might have been. "I'm just
somebody who likes to debunk things when there are alternate
explanations," he says, and he has not seen anything at the
museum that he does not believe could be explained in some
other way.

If Richmond is home to any ghosts at all, of course, it would
certainly be reasonable that some of them might haunt the
"Old Stone House," the oldest extant building in what is one
of the oldest cities in the country. None of the sites in Richmond where Poe actually lived or worked still exist, and the
museum is located in a collection of four contiguous buildings
that includes this aptly named structure, a 19th century carriage house (undergoing renovation during our visit in prepara-
tion for an exhibit of comic books and graphic novels inspired
by the author); a building constructed of bricks taken from the
house where Poe's mother died; and one other vintage house—
all clustered around an enclosed garden.

Poe did actually visit the Old Stone House at least once,
when as a boy he was part of the honor guard that accompanied

the Marquis de Lafayette on a tour of the city that stopped there. It is located just a few blocks from the home in which he grew up and the offices of the *Southern Literary Messenger,* the newspaper that gave him his first opportunity to write professionally, primarily as a literary critic.

His commentary on other peoples' work aside, anyone familiar with the development of English-language literature knows that the fiction works of Poe are among the most influential produced in America, particularly upon the genres of horror, mystery, science fiction, and poetry. A number of first-edition copies of the author's works are on display at the museum, including an 1845 edition of *The Raven and Other Poems;* a textbook on conchology that became a bestseller and led to accusations of plagiarism when it was discovered he wrote only its introduction; a facsimile of his first book, *Tamerlane,* a failure when it was released in 1827 but now one of the rarest and most valuable pieces of American literature; an original handwritten manuscript of the mysterious prose poem "Siope"; and the edition of *Godey's Lady's Book* in which Poe's scandalous and highly popular "Literati of New York City" appeared.

The Edgar Allan Poe Museum is also home to the largest collection of "Poeana," as its stewards term it, in the world. Such artifacts include the bed he slept in as a child, a walking stick that he inadvertently left in Richmond just a few weeks before his death, the key to the trunk containing his meager belongings, and a lock of hair posthumously clipped from his head by a friend.

This museum is much more than a collection of books and memorabilia, however, and visitors to it are made cognizant of the fact that there are people who have been profoundly affected by his words to the extent that they would be moved to memorialize the author who penned them. To whit, the Poe Museum was established less as a museum than as a shrine. Nowhere is that more clear than in the "Enchanted Garden," as the site's organizers dub it, a garden enclosed by the museum's buildings that has been one of the place's most attractive features since it was opened by the Poe Foundation in 1922.

Indeed, Poe considered gardens to be one of the highest forms of artistic expression, and it is thus appropriate that the centerpiece of the museum dedicated to him should be a garden inspired by his works in general and by the poem "To One in Paradise" in particular. Its features include plants, arrangements, a fountain, and other elements that can be found in the author's various works, along with a columned arcade made of bricks from the old *Southern Literary Messenger* offices that contains a bust of the author. Overall, it is certainly a pleasant and fitting tribute to Poe and probably an unparalleled spot to read or meditate upon his works. The garden is also a popular local

The Enchanted Garden at the Poe Museum

venue for weddings, some nineteen of which were held in it last year, Semtner said.

An air funereal as well as matrimonial permeates the museum, of course, and one of the exhibits in the museum points to how Poe's death is as much of a mystery as anything he ever wrote about and that its cause remains unclear to this day. Causes suggested over the more than a century and a half since his October 7, 1849, demise in Baltimore, Maryland— most based on successive developments in forensic medicine and many of them contradictory—have included being beaten to death (1857 and 1998), epilepsy (1874 and 1999), dipsomania (1921), heart problems (1926 and 1997), toxic disorder (1970), hypoglycemia (1977), diabetes (1977), alcohol dehydrogenase (1984), porphyria (1989), delirium tremens (1992), rabies (1996), and carbon monoxide poisoning (1999).

With as strange and mysterious a life and death as Poe is reputed to have had—something that was overstated to a great extent in the years after he died—organizers of local ghost tours would obviously be missing an opportunity if they did not include the Edgar Allan Poe Museum as one of their stops.

Semtner says that a lot of the tour guides say they're frightened of something upstairs in the carriage house. "Sometimes they claim to hear footsteps upstairs when they're downstairs," he said. Birds walking on the roof or acorns rolling down the roof, Semtner believess, are more likely explanations (although the oak tree that once produced those troublesome acorns is no longer there).

Such tours also stop outside the carriage house, Semtner says, where their participants are told that in photographs taken of one of its windows they can sometimes see the face of a child.

People have also experienced other evidence of what they believe are hauntings inside the various buildings, and there are other museum staff members, Semtner says—including a

woman who also guides local ghost tours—who would swear
the place is haunted.

"At the top of the stairs [in the carriage house] there's a little
bedroom display, and some of our tour guides are afraid to go
into it at night, because they have to go into the bedroom, turn
on the light, and then lock the door behind themselves," Semtner says. "One of our guides says she would leave the downstairs
door open so she could run out when she was afraid."

Ghost stories associated with the site generally involve children and would thus not seem to have any connection to Poe at
all (whose interest in children seems to have been directed primarily at his cousin Virginia Clemm, whom he married when
she was thirteen and he was twenty-six). Semtner also says there
are no records of any children having died in the house. As my
mother pointed out, of course, children regularly died from
any number of causes prior to the industrial age in America.
Records of such deaths, if they ever existed, might not still survive, and it is not unreasonable to think that children might con-
stitute a relatively large proportion of the ghosts in certain kinds
of places, such as family homes. Many of the odd occurrences
people have experienced at the museum are, in fact, prankish or
childlike in character, Semtner says, such as feeling their ears
flicked or having small objects tossed at the backs of their heads
when no one else is present.

"One fellow who was upstairs by himself [in the carriage
house] claimed he was pinched," for example, Semtner says.
And just within the past few years, he says, guests at weddings
in the garden have claimed to have seen children playing in it
even when it is clear that no living ones were actually there.

Semtner also says that a number of professional ghosthunting groups have conducted experiments in the museum and
generally determined it was haunted, but he is dismissive of
their methodology, which he brands as flawed and unscientific

(a standard he seems committed to, his background as an artist rather than a scientist notwithstanding).

Indeed, Semtner—who is often the first person to arrive at the museum, sometimes while it is still somewhat dark—says he has personally experienced a number of anomalies that are almost classical in their association with haunted places. These have included hearing the courtyard door to the Old Stone House opening and closing in the early morning hours when he was the only one at the site and having his knocks upon walls mimicked from elsewhere in the house when no other people were there. Because these effects cannot be reproduced in accordance with the standards of the scientific method, however, Semtner says he is not willing to accept them as evidence of a supernatural presence.

While that would seem to be an unduly high standard to a more naturalistic ghosthunter like myself, my mother and I certainly did not witness any evidence of hauntings while we were at the museum—although it is not likely that we would have anyway on a short visit during the day. And, while the identities of the spectral urchins some believe to haunt the place are at the least uncertain, it is a pretty sure bet that there is one unquiet spirit that does not haunt the place: Edgar Allan Poe, who could hardly be anything but pleased with this heartfelt memorial to his life and works and to the somewhat macabre reputation it has acquired.

CHAPTER 11

Trapezium House
PETERSBURG

The architectural oddity was built by Charles O'Hara, whose West Indian servant convinced him that spirits could inhabit only right-angled buildings. So, the O'Hara house has no right angles at all. None of the walls are parallel, doors and windows are all framed crooked, and the stairs and floorboards are cut at a slant.

—Dennis William Hauck,
Haunted Places: The National Directory

IF ANY MUNICIPALITY IN VIRGINIA is likely to be
haunted, it is almost certainly Petersburg, a crumbling, indus-
trialized, antebellum sprawl along the banks of the Appomattox
River that is notable both as a historical city and as the scene of
one of the bloodiest massacres in U.S. history.

On July 30, 1864, U.S. Army engineers attempted to break
through the defenses of the besieged Confederate city by detonat-
ing a massive quantity of explosives in a tunnel dug beneath the
city's fortifications. The explosion created a 135-foot-wide crater
and instantly pulverized as many as 350 rebel soldiers. Confused
and lackluster Union commanders squandered this initial success
by ordering an entire division of troops into the crater, rather than
marching around it. They where butchered by the quickly rally-
ing Southerners, who seized control of the high ground above the
hole. Some 5,300 of the Federal troops were killed, wounded, or
captured before the ill-fated assault was abandoned.

Hunting for the ghosts of poorly led soldiers who died to
no good end seemed a little too grim for me, however, as my
wife, Diane, and I passed through Petersburg a couple days after
Christmas 2007. Our plan, rather, was to visit a much more
classic haunted site, a 190-year-old building known locally as
the Trapezium House. We were en route to Atlanta, Georgia,
and hoped to make the most of our time by spending the night
at the Quality Inn at the Washington Street exit off I-95, visiting the Trapezium House the next day, and getting on the road
again by mid-morning.

Our ghost hunt was not to begin auspiciously, however—a
realization which began to dawn on us when we had trouble
finding the motel. Eventually going into the office of what looked
like an abandoned Rodeway Inn at approximately the right location, I was greeted by the young female clerk sitting behind the
counter and, on the wall behind her, the word "Y INN" (the let-
ters "QUALIT" having long ago fallen away). Had I not reserved

and paid for a room in advance, we would certainly have moved on to another place.

It is almost inconceivable that this rotting, sepulchral, nearly empty collection of multilevel wings at the edge of the interstate, which we would come to call the *Yinn,* was itself not haunted. It looked like the kind of setting that Snoop Dog might have chosen if he had directed *The Shining.* Yes, the seemingly unnatural cold that permeated our room could possibly be attributed to the innkeeper's indifference to the comfort of the guests checked into a mere half dozen of the dilapidated estab-lishment's hundreds of room, as frigid air was all we could coax out of the climate control vents. Beyond that, however, the deso-late edifice evoked spectral images of failed Willy Lomans dead of self-inflicted wounds and urbanized folk who had met violent ends in drug deals gone bad in its bleak little rooms. We spent a grim, fitful night, during which I looked out often to make sure our SUV was still there, and we had an intimate awareness of everything that rattled by on I-95.

Nothing induced us to delay our departure in the morn-ing, and we arrived ten minutes early for our meeting at the Trapezium House, a mere seven-tenths of a mile away. It was located a few blocks down Market Street, the apparent line of demarcation between a largely industrial area that stretched from there to the interstate and a neighborhood of historical mansions that extended away from it. I had scouted out the site the night before, and taken a few pictures of it, but daylight clearly revealed to me the source of the three-story brick build-ing's primary name—namely, a four-sided structure having no parallel walls. I was photographing the exterior when the cur-rent owner arrived. I had called him the week before, and he had graciously agreed to meet my wife and me at the house and to tell us what he knew about it.

Irishman Charles O'Hara—who is referred to only by this title in any source I could find—purchased the lot the house is on in 1816 and completed construction of it the following year. According to local legend, a West Indian slave owned by O'Hara convinced him that evil spirits are able to dwell in right angles and, accordingly, advised him to build his home without any. Why O'Hara believed this, and why he was concerned about his house becoming a harborage for evil spirits, is lost to the ages, if it is indeed true at all. A more austere, latter-day explanation holds that he was merely building to the shape of his lot and that similar structures were once common in Petersburg (although none are extant today). In any event, the original owner is the source of one of the other local names for the place, the Charles O'Hara House.

Beyond his supposed preoccupation with evil spirits, O'Hara was reputed to be more than mildly eccentric and to have a habit of heavy drinking (but this latter detail may actually be an unfair embellishment that seems to be almost universally applied to Irishmen in tales of this sort). It is, however, his reputed practice of keeping in his house a little menagerie—which is said to have included a monkey, a parrot, and a number of white rats—that gained the place yet another local nickname: the Rat Castle.

Some believe that whatever demons haunted O'Hara in life and encouraged his various eccentricities also kept his unquiet spirit from passing on after death—and that the unparallel angles of his home which might have kept other spirits out of the house inadvertently served to trap his own ghost within it. The Trapezium House is cited as a haunted site by a number of authorities, including *Haunted Places: The National Directory* and the official "Virginia is for Lovers" Web site.

The current owner of the house, a sagacious man who it would be fair to characterize as "sober as a judge," is a bit more skeptical.

Oliver A. Pollard Jr. is, in fact, a retired Circuit Court Judge with thirty-six years on the bench, and a fifth-generation native of Petersburg, which his family has dwelled in since 1740. (He is also the picture of a Southern gentleman and, apparently, too refined to have even noticed something as coarse and awful as the *Yinn*, which, despite its close proximity and his long ties to the community, Pollard seemed to be completely unaware of.)

The Society for the Preservation of Petersburg Antiquities had acquired the property in the 1930s, and in recent years the city had operated it as a tourist attraction, opening it on request and sending a guide from another site to unlock it and lead visitors through it. By the turn of the millennium, however, the municipality had too many such minor sites to effectively administer and thus sold them off to private parties, with easements dictating that they be properly preserved and open to the public a certain number of days per year. Pollard was thus able to purchase the Trapezium House in 2002, and has used it since that time as an office, as a studio for the painting to which he has increasingly turned since retirement, and for storage.

Pollard does not reside in the Trapezium House, and that might account for why he has not noticed any evidence of haunting. He might also have the kind of temperament that is inclined not to notice such things. He is willing to admit, however, that he has heard stories about the house and that someone close to him has reacted adversely to it.

That someone was his now-deceased Jack Russell Terrier, Russ, who would refuse to go up the stairs to the second floor—the level upon which O'Hara lived. The poor dog would just cower by the front door until his master was ready to leave.

Pollard also concedes that O'Hara does seem to have been odd, and that he employed measures in his construction of the Trapezium House that go far beyond the need to accommodate the shape of an irregular lot.

"You can see it's built in the shape of a trapezium," Pollard said, pointing out various features of the ground level as he spoke from the old, swiveling jury chair that he uses at his ground floor work station. "There are no right angles. If you look at the side of the staircase, you can see that it is offset. The lot is somewhat trapezoid in shape, but he did carry it to extremes. There's no need to not put the fireplace in the center of the wall. Also, the staircase is cattywampus and the floorboards are cut on oblique angles. Even the bricks are a little cockeyed."

I could readily see everything Pollard pointed out, and, irregularly shaped lot or not, O'Hara had indeed applied considerable effort and additional expense to avoid the incorporation of any ninety-degree angle.

Pollard concluded our interview with a brief tour of the house, during which my wife and I availed ourselves of the opportunity to enjoy his collection of predominantly Impressionist-style paintings—including a small, affectionate one of Russ, the Jack Russell Terrier—and to take some photographs. During our time in the house, neither of us noticed anything profoundly out of the ordinary beyond the strange construction, although toward the end of the tour I did experience a mild feeling of discomfort similar to the sensation of having someone look over my shoulder. We presently stepped outside and then chatted with the judge at the door for a few more minutes before walking across the street to our car and resuming our journey.

Rain and poor driving conditions harried us all the way to Atlanta, and it was not until two nights later, in the city of a different O'Hara, that I had the opportunity to download my photographs and check the quality of my interview tape. To say that I was stunned by the results would be an understatement.

Most of the more-than-fifty digital photographs I had taken were pretty much what I expected: some were better or worse than others; a few were fairly good and of publication quality; a few were worthless. Two, however, revealed effects unlike any I've seen in the thousands of digital pictures I have taken over the years.

One of the photos of the exterior of the Trapezium House— the very first one, in fact, that I had taken the night we arrived in Petersburg—was warped and distorted, as if the space and light between me and it had somehow been twisted widdershins.

Bent, ghost images of the house looked as if they were being twisted away from it. None of the other photos I took at that time looked in any way irregular.

The second odd photo was one I took during our last few minutes in the house, of the stairway as it descended from the uppermost level of the house. Centered along the upper edge of the image, was a wispy, gray mass, located as if it were moving from one floor of the building to another.

And on my audio tape, a distinct chirping noise is obvious at two points during a thirty-minute period—the first right after I asked Pollard if the house was haunted and almost in response to his skepticism on that point.

There are no clear words on that tape other than the ones uttered by me, my wife, or Pollard, and there is nothing indisputable in the odd characteristics of those two photographs. Suffice it to say, however, that I believe those anomalies suggest the presence of something out of the ordinary in the Trapezium House—and that someone other than the judge may very well have been trying to answer my questions on that point.

A wispy, wraithlike form manifested itself along the upper edge of this image taken from the third floor of the Trapezium House and down into its stairway.

CHAPTER 12

Wreck of the Old 97

DANVILLE

It's a mighty rough road from Lynchburg to Danville,
And the lie was a three-mile grade,
It was on that grade that he lost his air brakes,
And you see what a jump that she made.

He was going down the grade making 90 miles an hour,
When his whistle began to scream,
He was found in that wreck with his hand on the throttle,
He was scalded to death by the steam.

—"The Wreck of the Old 97"

ON SEPTEMBER 27, 1903, the train known as the "Old 97" flew off a bridge near Danville, Virginia, and smashed into the ravine below, horribly killing eleven people who had been on board and injuring seven others. It was one of the worst train wrecks in the history of the state and, within a few years, became one of the most famous in the country as the result of a song about it that became the first record in the United States to sell more than a million copies.

Mail-and-express train No. 97, consisting of four cars and locomotive No. 1102, was one of the "Fast Mail" trains run by the Southern Railway under contract to the U.S. Postal Service. It ran 640 miles from Washington, D.C., to Atlanta, Georgia, and was on the leg that went from Monroe, Virginia—176 miles southwest of Washington—to Spencer, North Carolina, a route that passed through Danville. No. 97 had started its run late and was an hour behind schedule when thirty-three-year-old engineer Joseph A. "Steve" Broady climbed aboard at Monroe for the leg into Spencer, another 166 miles down the track, where it would pick up a new crew. For every minute it was late into Atlanta, Southern Railway would forfeit a substantial amount of money to the Postal Service, which would not reflect well on the engineers, whether it was their fault or not. And so, Broady ran the train hard, and tried to make up for lost time.

Despite the folksy name commonly attributed to it, No. 97 was not actually that old when it met its end, and was one of the workhorses of the Southern line. Its engine was one of the best available, a ten-wheeled model produced by the Baldwin Locomotive Works. It carried no passengers, just eighteen crewmen and postal workers, and earned its keep by fulfilling the terms of its owner's $140,000 annual contract to carry mail south from the nation's capital to Atlanta.

While the claim that it was "the fastest regularly scheduled train in the world" might have been a bit of an exaggeration, No. 97 did maintain an average speed of nearly forty miles per hour and had a reputation for never being late. The normal time allotted for the run from Monroe to Spencer was four hours and fifteen minutes, which the train accomplished by maintaining an average speed of 39 miles per hour. If Broady wanted No. 97 to be back on schedule by the time he reached his destination, he would need to cut the time to just three hours and fifteen minutes and to run the train at an average speed of at least fifty-one miles per hour—which would be a trick, to say the least, in the rolling country ahead of him, which included many steep grades and tight curves. Signs posted along the route warned engineers to watch their speeds.

Broady did his best, blazing through at least one intermediate stop normally made during the run. It is not known for certain how fast he was driving No. 97 as it approached Stillhouse Trestle, the bridge that would carry it across the Dan River into Danville. Witnesses claimed it was going anywhere from thirty-five to eighty miles per hour, with the most likely estimates being closer to about fifty miles per hour. Any of those speeds but the very lowest would have been too fast for the curve leading down the steep, three-mile grade onto the bridge.

As he approached the curve, Broady discovered with horror that he did not have enough air pressure in his brakes to slow the train sufficiently. In desperation, he reversed the engine in an attempt to lock its wheels so as to slow or stop the train and sounded its shrieking whistle, in order to alert the crew to apply the hand brakes on the cars. It was all futile, however, and as train No. 97 struck the curve at high speed, it flew off the tracks, splintering a telegraph pole and tearing through the wires that ran parallel to the tracks. It then went soaring out into the air, its whistle screaming as if in mortal terror.

Engine 1102 traveled about one-hundred feet through open space and then crashed into the rocky creek bed in the ravine forty-five feet below the trestle. Its four cars followed and smashed into it in turn, piling up onto the wrecked engine and each other.

Of the eighteen people on board, ten were killed in the wreck, including all five of the train crew, four postal clerks, and a "safe locker" employed by the railway; seven were injured, all of them postal clerks, one of whom succumbed to his wounds nine days later; and one, an express messenger, escaped without being hurt at all. The injuries to the killed and wounded were horrific, and many of the victims were dying when people arrived at the scene of the wreck and tried to pull victims out of it.

"The three men in the engine were so badly scalded by hot water and steam that they were all the same color," witness J. E. Lester recalled years later. "It was a horrible experience." The two mangled and scalded firemen had been ejected from the left side of the engine and appeared to have died quickly. Broady was still alive when he was flung from the engine and landed in the creek bed next to it, but was horribly injured; his skin peeled off as witness John Wiley pulled him away from the wreck and

No. 97 flew off the tracks and careened into a creek bed forty-five feet below after hiting a dangerous curve at high speed.

he died right afterward.

In the aftermath of the disaster, Southern Railway disavowed any responsibility for the wreck, claiming that it had not encouraged Broady to make up lost time and that he had been going too fast and was alone to blame. It is the railway that would have been penalized if the train had arrived late at its final destination, of course, and it is a sure bet that its engineers were always under pressure to ensure that No. 97 arrived in Atlanta on time. A coroner's inquest held in Danville three days after the tragedy determined that its cause was excessive speed, but allowed that it could not say whether that speed was the result of human error or mechanical failure.

In the years following the wreck of the No. 97, people began to see strange activity in the ravine below the bridge, including what appeared to be lantern lights moving around in it, as if carried by people searching for the survivors of a crash. Stillhouse Trestle was used for another dozen years after the wreck, until the Southern Railway mainline was shifted about a mile east in 1915. However, even after the trestle was removed and the ravine became so overgrown with vegetation that people could no longer pass easily through it, the phantasmal lights were still seen. And, even though trains no longer passed anywhere near the site, people nearby were sometimes shocked to hear the shriek of a train whistle near where No. 97 sounded its last blast.

People also began to talk about "the Curse of the Old 97," which seemed to strike any endeavor whose owners sought to benefit from the legacy of the misfortune. One of the most well-known examples of this is the case of the Old 97 Steak House. This eatery was established by an aspiring restaurateur in nearby Witt, Virginia, in the renovated and expanded Fall Creek Depot, which the No. 97 had sped past just minutes before reaching Stillhouse Trestle. It was a going concern in the early 1990s but, after it burned down mysteriously several years ago, it was never reopened.

My wife and I arrived in Danville on the evening of January 30, 2007, checked into a hotel on a hill just off Route 58 overlooking the Dan River valley, and immediately started asking around about the wreck of the Old 97 and ghost stories associated with it. Ironically, almost every single person we talked to—including Colie Walker, night cook at the restaurant affiliated with the hotel we stayed at, who we chatted with the most that evening—was familiar with the stories, but also told us that the site had been quiet for a long time and that if we were looking for ghosts we should instead visit nearby Berry Hill Road (which we did, it being the subject of its own chapter in this book). No one was denying that the site was haunted, mind you—a widespread attitude that surprised us—just that nothing had apparently happened at it for awhile.

One of our original sources of information about places associated with the wreck was the official "Virginia is for Lovers" tourism Web site, which mentioned two relevant points of interest: the site of the wreck itself, marked by a historic placard, and a mural on a building across the river that commemorated the wreck and the deaths of the railway and postal workers killed in it. The morning after we arrived in Danville, we got up and headed down Route 58 to the bridge that would take us across the Dan River into the historic downtown of Danville, where we found the mural painted on the side of the building at 310 Main Street.

A visit to the forty-foot-tall, seventy-five-foot-wide mural completed in 2005, seemed an appropriate way to set the tone for our investigation that day. The mural consisted of three elements, the largest of which depicted No. 97 in all its original glory. A smaller panel to its right showed the remains of the engine in the ravine beneath Stillhouse Trestle. From an inset oval panel, depictions of the five crewmen killed in the wreck stared out at us.

From there, we followed directions to the address where, according to the tourism Web site, the wreck had occurred and was marked. These took us several miles to the west of town, back across the river to its north side, and up a hill to a visitor's center. Something did not seem right, and we certainly could not correlate anything in the surrounding hilly terrain with what we had read about the wreck.

Suffice it to say that the address on the Web site had been wrong, and that the ladies working in the visitor's center pointed us in the right direction. We still needed to make one more stop for directions while working our way back down Route 58 east toward where we had started, but ultimately ended up in the little parking lot of a Supertest gas station, which stood just a short distance from the historic marker we were seeking and overlooked the ravine over which Stillhouse Trestle had once crossed. We were not far from the bridge we had taken into Danville a little earlier and almost directly across the river from where the mural was located.

Other than the historic marker—which incorrectly identifies the number of killed as nine, rather then the actual eleven— there is not too much to see at the site today, which bears little resemblance to how it looked in 1903. Diane dutifully waited in the car while I took some pictures, clambered part of the way down into the ravine, and then went into the little gas station store to ask some questions. The man working behind the counter just laughed when I asked him if he had ever seen anything that might suggest the site was haunted.

Whatever ghosts are associated with the wreck of No. 97 are, it would seem, quiet for the moment, and perhaps they have gone on to their eternal rest and will never be heard from again. The site where the ill-fated train met its end is, nonetheless, a desolate one, and I would not be at all surprised to see lights moving around in the tangled ravine some starless night, or to hear again the spectral shriek of a whistle on the anniversary of the catastrophe.

COAST

**VIRGINIA:
COASTAL
AREA**

Maryland

ACCOMACK

CHESAPEAKE BAY

MATHEWS

GLOUCESTER

CHARLES CITY

JAMES CITY

NORTHAMPTON

YORK

NEWPORT NEWS

SURRY

HAMPTON

ISLE OF WIGHT

SUFFOLK

VIRGINIA BEACH

CHESAPEAKE

ATLANTIC
OCEAN

Assateague Island
Assateague Lighthouse

Chincoteague Island
1848 Island Manor House

Hampton
Fort Monroe

Williamsburg
Colonial Williamsburg

CHAPTER 13

Assateague Lighthouse
ASSATEAGUE ISLAND

Years went by. And more years. Changes came to Assateague. The red men came. The white men came. The white men built a lighthouse to warn ships of dangerous reefs. They built a handful of houses and a white church. But soon the houses stood empty. The people moved their homes and their church to nearby Chincoteague Island, for Assateague belonged to the wild things—to the wild birds that nested on it, and the wild ponies whose ancestors had lived on it since the days of the Spanish galleon.

—Marguerite Henry, *Misty of Chincoteague*

FEW IF ANY PEOPLE lived on Assateague Island, a thirty-
seven-mile-long barrier island separating mainland Virginia
from the Atlantic Ocean, when a Spanish galleon ran aground
off its coast on September 5, 1720, and it is likely that nobody
ashore witnessed the wreck. Its arrival, nonetheless, was to have
a lasting impact on the history and lore of the island.

La Galga, "The Greyhound," was one of seven ships in a treasure fleet laden with gold, silver, and other valuables bound from
Havana to Cadiz, Spain. When it ran onto the shallows off the
coast of Assateague—just two ship lengths from land, according
to the testimony of its captain—the crew attempted to lighten it
by driving overboard the horses that were part of its cargo. Five
of the sailors followed their example, leapt into the sea, and tried
to make it to the shore. Since then, the island has been haunted
both by the descendants of the horses that managed to swim
ashore—and by the ghosts of the Spaniards who did not.

Assateague had had a relatively quiet history up to that point.
Indians had come to the island on a seasonal basis to hunt and
fish for as long as anyone could remember but had established no
permanent communities on the island. The horses were among
some of its first fulltime inhabitants in historical times (there
being evidence for permanent Clovis culture settlements until
about 11,000 years ago). And, sometime in the decade prior to
the wreck of La Galga, the pirate Edward Teach—better known
as Blackbeard—is believed to have come to the island, and perhaps to have buried some of his ill-gotten treasure there.

By 1764, the number of horses on the island far exceeded
the sparse population of perhaps two dozen human inhabitants,
most of them herders and fishermen. From about that time
onward, people began to tell stories about ghostly presences on
the island. Some claimed that the shadowy figures that could
be seen moving noiselessly across the dunes on moonlit nights
were the shades of Spanish sailors killed in the legendary wreck
off their shores. Others believed that the ghosts that haunted

Assateague were those of pirates who had fallen afoul of the fearsome Blackbeard and had been slain by him in one of the violent altercations typical among buccaneer crews. Yet others held that the horses, which could be seen slipping wraithlike through the tangled thickets of the island, were the reincarnated spirits of those who had died on the island.

About one hundred years after the horses arrived, the U.S. government decided that the mid-Atlantic coastline was not adequately protected from offshore hazards—the nearest lighthouses being the ones at Cape Charles, Virginia, nearly seventy miles to the south and Cape Henlopen, Delaware, about eighty miles to the north—and that the dangerous, knife-like shoals off the shores of Assateague required that a lighthouse be built on the island.

Assateague's first lighthouse, a cylindrical white brick tower some forty-five feet high, twenty-two feet wide at its base, and ten-and-one-half feet wide at its crown, was built in 1833 and became active on May 5 of that year. It was lit by a "Lewis Lamp," consisting of eleven oil-burning lamps that, with a series of fourteen-inch reflectors, were mounted in a chandelier-style arrangement. A two-room brick house for the keeper was constructed in conjunction with the lighthouse.

Seven years after it began operating, Assateague's first lighthouse keeper, David Watson, who had tended the tower by himself since it had been commissioned, died under circumstances that to this day are still somewhat unclear. Some believe that his spirit lingers yet at the site, automatically continuing in death the unchanging routines he followed in life. However, since the tower he tended has been replaced with a much larger one, one could wonder whether the shade might not be confused or even irritated by his altered surroundings.

Indeed, Assateague's first lighthouse was almost immediately deemed to be inadequate, and at its fairly short height was unable to project a warning beam far enough out to sea to warn mariners of shoals that extended out as far as twelve miles. An 1852 report by the Lighthouse Board recommended that it be replaced as soon as possible. Government did not move very quickly in that era, however, and, by the time the Civil War began nine years later, all that had been accomplished was the construction of a wharf and a plank road. Further work was suspended until resolution of the conflict between North and South.

Supported by a U.S. Navy base on a nearby island, Union troops were stationed on the island and guarded the lighthouse from the depredations of Confederate saboteurs. The area was, by all accounts, a hotbed of naval intrigue throughout the war and the military presence was by no means extraneous.

"The British would actually sail ships into the north section and down Chincoteague Harbor, where they would meet Confederate troops, retrofit the ships, and leave as Southern battleships," Jerry Prewitt, proprietor of the 1848 Island Manor House on nearby Chincoteague Island, told me when we chatted about the history of the area.

Construction of the new lighthouse began the year after the war ended and it was completed, along with a new duplex keeper's bungalow, in 1867. In the process, the older structure was torn down and probably incorporated into the foundations of the new one. Two keepers were assigned to this larger lighthouse (a number that was increased to three in 1876 and then four in 1909, and decreased to three in 1918 and then two again in 1922; in 1933, the lighthouse was automated and remains so today, requiring no keeper).

The new lighthouse was 142 feet high and was originally covered with a brick-colored cement wash that was replaced by the U.S. Coast Guard with its current distinctive red-and-white striped pattern in 1968.

For its light, Assateague's new lighthouse was equipped with a powerful array of crystals called a Fresnel lens—a marked improvement over the somewhat second-rate system that had served the earlier lighthouse—that was classified as "first-order," meaning that it was of the largest sort available (by comparison, the previous light had been a third-order lens).

A village grew up north of the lighthouse at the base of the dunes, where it was protected from storms and wind. It consisted of perhaps three dozen dwellings, most of them relatively primitive wood-framed structures on brick pilings. A school was built for the required minimum of forty students in 1890, and the Union Baptist Church of Chincoteague opened a meeting house for Wednesday services in 1919. Most of the village's inhabitants earned a living by clamming, fishing, or oystering, and some worked at a short-lived fish-processing plant during the period 1912 to 1928.

A spiral staircase provides access to the various levels of the 42-foot-tall Assateague Lighthouse.

Assateague Village began to decline from about 1922 onward, when amenities like electricity, telephone, and public water became available on Chincoteague and began luring people away from the island. Contributing to dissatisfaction with life on Assateague was Samuel B. Field, a major property owner who made it difficult for inhabitants to move around the island by preventing them from crossing his land. When the lighthouse was automated in 1933 and its keepers left, the last of the villagers followed suit, leaving behind just a couple of die-hards.

Except for a few inhabitants, like Field, Assateague was once again the realm of horses and ghosts and would have felt nearly as mysterious and isolated as it had in decades past, until a bridge was built out to it from Chincoteague in 1962, and tourists began to visit it in the summer and on weekends. The island remains hauntingly wild and beautiful even to this day, and it is easy to imagine that the spirits of those who have lost their lives upon its shores might yet lurk within the tangled copses of its forests or drift on starry nights along its silvery dunes.

"The area around the wreck of La Galga is very eerie," John Amrhein, author of The Hidden Galleon, a book about the wreck of that Spanish ship, told me when we discussed the subject of ghosts on Assateague. "Five people died, not on ship, but drowned coming ashore."

"During my many visits and while writing the book I always felt that I was being watched and helped," Amrhein said of his extensive research. "The captain and crew want their story to be told."

It would be fair to say that my wife and I certainly felt that a mysterious presence might be nearby during our visit to Assateague in March 2008. It was then prior to the start of the tourist season, and we did not encounter very many other people during our stops at the island's various visitors' centers or our

Although automated and unmanned, Assateague Lighthouse is still operational today. Nearby Chincoteague Island can be seen through the window.

hike along its seashore or wooded trails, from which we were able to spot small herds of the feral horses for which Assateague is most famous.

Our visit to the island also took place before the lighthouse was open to the public for the year, but we were fortunate enough to make the acquaintance of Laurel Wilkerson, a ranger with the U.S. Fish and Wildlife Service who works at its facilities on the island. Her agency, in conjunction with the Coast Guard, administers the site, and she graciously agreed to give us a tour of the lighthouse and told us a great deal about the history of both it and the island.

One of the first things we wondered about was why the lighthouse is located so far from the Atlantic shoreline, which it is intended to help make more navigable, and the answer she gave was very interesting. In short, barrier islands shift over the years and, depending on the conditions to which they are subjected, can shrink, grow, or change shape. When the lighthouse was built in 1867, it was on a bluff overlooking the Atlantic. Today, it is five miles from the ocean and separated from it by land that did not exist 140 years ago and has gradually built up since that time, much of it now being covered by meadow and woods.

We did not see anything ghostlike during the time we spent in the tower, and nothing strange later turned up in the photographs I took while we were there (although the crawlspace above the entryway was definitely very creepy). But it was an oddly melancholy site, and it was easy to see how a solitary lighthouse keeper might see almost anything during the long hours of watches during the night, or how his spirit might perhaps unconsciously continue its lonely vigil even into the afterlife.

During the years she has worked at Assateague, Laurel said she has not experienced anything definitely paranormal, and she could not say for sure whether or not she believes the lighthouse is haunted. She did say, however, that some odd things have been known to happen at it. One thing that occurred a number of times just prior to our visit, for example, involves the entrance to the tower, for which there are only a few strictly accounted-for sets of keys and which the Coast Guard and Fish and Wildlife Service personnel make a stringent effort to keep locked. Nonetheless, despite their best efforts, this door is often found inexplicably unlocked or open.

Who is more mystified and annoyed—the staff members who have to keep locking the door or the shade of a former lighthouse keeper, perhaps that of keeper David Watson himself, who keeps unlocking it—is an open question.

CHAPTER 14

1848 Island Manor House
CHINCOTEAGUE ISLAND

After washing up on the sandy wetlands, these restless souls yearn for the shelter of the dark ground, and some may reach out desperately to the living for help in reaching eternal rest... Delmarva has a large number of ghosts because phantoms cannot get off the peninsula, cannot travel across water, as the old superstition says.

—Ed and Kathleen Okonowicz, *Crying in the Kitchen*

THERE IS ABSOLUTELY NO DOUBT in the mind of Jerry Prewitt, proprietor of the 1848 Island Manor House, that his establishment is haunted by no less than three ghosts, and many of his guests have sensed the presence of one or more of them with no prompting from him. But far from ever being compelled to run screaming from the house in terror, he says, he has come to enjoy a sense of security with his spectral boarders.

My wife and I spent a weekend at Jerry's inn on Chincoteague Island in mid-March 2008, as part of a ghosthunting expedition that included investigation of the nearby Assateague Lighthouse. Jerry and I had actually crossed paths some fourteen months earlier, when he attended some of my historical lectures during a cruise on the *Regal Princess* through the Panama Canal in January 2007, a coincidence we discovered when we began talking about my visit to the island. We thus had the pleasure of meeting Jerry for the second time during our trip.

Diane and I had wanted to visit the historic island for many years, but despite having lived in the Old Dominion for nearly two decades, had never found the opportunity to do so. That is not as strange as it might sound at first, however, as the town of Chincoteague is almost as far from our home in Springfield, Virginia, as it could be and still be in the same state. And, because of the intervening Chesapeake Bay, the quickest way to reach it involved a drive that was predominantly through the adjoining state of Maryland and via its capital of Annapolis. And so, after a five-hour drive that began with a rush-hour slog around Washington, D.C.'s Capital Beltway, my wife and I completed our nearly two-hundred-mile trip to the island.

It was dark by the time we reached Chincoteague, and we could see the lights of the town twinkling ahead of us as we crossed the four-and-one-half mile-long series of causeways and bridges that both link it with the mainland and emphasize its sense of seclusion from the world at large. Indeed, Chincoteague has remained relatively isolated since its first white settlers arrived on the island April 1, 1671. From then until 1922—when the causeway that connects the island with the nearby Delmarva

Peninsula was opened—it could be reached only by boat. It was largely a lawless place in its early years, with no government or police, and is rumored to have been a refuge for former convicts and other ruffians. Mail service to the island was not established until 1854, when its first post office was opened.

Chincoteague takes its name from the tribe of Gingo-Teague Indians who were dwelling on the seven-mile-long, two-mile-wide barrier island in the 17th century and who, appropriately, called it "Beautiful Land Across the Water." Its first white settlers and many of their descendants alike have supported themselves by farming corn, potatoes, and strawberries for their own consumption, and harvesting clams, fish, oysters (including a succulent local variety, the "Chincoteague salty"), and salt from the sea both for themselves and trade with the mainland.

By the mid-1800s, the island had become too populous for its inhabitants to support themselves primarily through farming and, as trade became more important, the town itself began to grow. Around this time the steamboat *Chincoteague* was commissioned to carry passengers and freight to and from the island, departing Franklin City on the mainland and going back and forth to the island throughout the summer. Stores, hotels, and churches began to open along the streets of the quiet fishing village, and a new wave of settlers from the mainland traveled to it.

Among the people flocking to the boom town were two affluent young gentlemen, merchant Joseph Kenny and Dr. Nathaniel Smith, who established themselves as some of the community's most prominent citizens. This prominence is evident in the grand home they cooperatively built on Main Street, about two-thirds of which have been incorporated into the 1848 Island Manor House.

Drawing on the Southern architectural tradition then prevalent throughout the mid-Atlantic region, Kenny and Smith constructed a grand residence in the form of a "Maryland 'T' House," popular in that era, that incorporated Georgian and Federalist design elements. Both remained prominent citizens, with Kenny in particular going on to serve as the town's elected postmaster when its sole post office was opened in 1854.

When Southern states began seceding from the United States in 1860, prior to the Civil War that broke out the following year, Chincoteague was exceptional in that it remained under Union control and its citizens faithful to the Stars and Stripes.

"That was because of our connection with the oyster and scallop and clam industry, which sold to Philadelphia, New York City, and Washington, D.C.," Jerry says.

Along with war came some small fame for Chincoteague: After Union forces that included many men from the island won a significant battle, the native oysters were served to some four thousand people at a victory celebration, and Chincoteague thereafter became known for them. The Island Manor House served as a Union infirmary during the war, and Dr. Smith himself treated Union troops during the conflict.

Kenny and Smith must certainly have been some of Chincoteague's most eligible bachelors in the postwar years, and both eventually married. First was the merchant, who married a young woman from Baltimore, Maryland, named Sarah. He was followed soon after by the doctor, who married another young woman from Baltimore named Juliet, who, perhaps not coincidentally, happened to be the sister of Sarah. Both couples dwelled under the roof of the home that had been so amicably shared by Kenny and Smith prior to their nuptials, but the sisters could not get along with each other, and the household was ultimately split in half—literally.

Workers built a new foundation next to the existing structure, and when it was complete the house was cut in two and one half was disconnected and painstakingly moved to the new location. The Kenny family remained in the original section, and the Smith family moved into the relocated one.

"If you look closely at the Island Manor House today you will see that one portion sits lower than the other since the new foundation was not built to the original height," Jerry says. "These houses were used as separate residences for many decades."

Construction on the causeway connecting Chincoteague with the mainland began in 1919. That was not soon enough, however, to be of use to the town in a great fire that broke out the following year, the same one in which the fledgling Volunteer Fire Department of Chincoteague was founded. Departments from the mainland were unable to assist in putting out the conflagration, and the town was nearly destroyed, with much of Main Street and many of the buildings along it succumbing to the flames.

Chincoteague survived but another major fire struck the town just four years later, in 1924. In response to this, some forty local women decided to form an auxiliary to the volunteer fire department and to hold an annual fundraiser to support the efforts of the firefighters.

The event that grew out of this resolution is today Chincoteague's great claim to fame and has been related to millions of readers in the classic children's tale *Misty of Chincoteague,* published by Marguerite Henry in 1946. Every year on the last Wednesday in July, a certain number of feral ponies are rounded up on nearby Assateague Island and swum across the channel separating it from Chincoteague. Pony Penning Day is celebrated the following day as the ponies are auctioned off at a carnival that includes bake sales and other means of raising money for the volunteer fire department. (Any of the ponies that do not sell are swum back to Assateague on Friday.)

Over the years, the annual festival increasingly began to attract people from around the country and to draw attention to the area's great natural beauty, its beaches, its wildlife, its seafood, it history, and its seclusion. Now, hundreds of thousands of visitors come to the island every year, swelling the ranks of its 4,500 regular inhabitants and supporting the dense collection of inns, hotels, restaurants, boutiques, and bookstores that fill the small downtown.

With demand growing for places to accommodate those visitors, some prospective innkeepers purchased the historic Kenny and Smith residences in the 1980s—the latter from the descendants of its original inhabitant—and converted it into one of the island's first bed-and-breakfasts, which they named the Little Traveler's Inn. They decided to reconnect the two homes and built the long sunroom that now unifies the structure.

New owners acquired the inn in the early 1990s and changed the name to the one it currently bears as both a tribute to the year it was built and to gentrify its image a little. They expanded the scope of the establishment, increasing the number of guest rooms to the eight the property currently has and adding the red brick courtyard—complete with rosebushes and a three-tired fountain—that now lies between the two wings.

Then, in 2003, Jerry and his partner Andrew Dawson took over the 1848 Island Manor House.

"I decided to go into business for myself and started looking for a bed-and-breakfast," says Jerry, who taught public school for six years in Kentucky and then went on to do corporate training in northern Virginia for four. "I had been to the eastern shore several times but had never been to Chincoteague until I actually came to look at property, and I loved Chincoteague and Assateague and [their] history."

The things real estate disclosure laws require people to reveal about a property when they sell it, however, do not include the presence of ghosts, and Jerry soon began to experience some strange things. He eventually came to the conclusion that three ghosts dwell within the 1848 Island Manor House, and that they are a little girl, a woman dressed as a Civil War-era nurse, and a middle-aged man with the attire and demeanor of a butler.

Jerry says his favorite is probably the little girl, who appears to be between seven and ten years of age. "She's our little prank-ster and enjoys playing chess. The reason I know that is when I'm here by myself and no one [else] has been here, I've actually seen [that] chess pieces have been moved, as if a game is in prog-ress," he says, referring to the chessboard in the sunroom.

Jerry is not alone in having experienced ghostly presences in the house, he says, and that many guests have as well. "Typi-cally after breakfast on their last day here," Jerry says, people who have experienced something out of the ordinary "will ask me if we have ghosts."

In particular, Jerry says, during his time at the inn at least five or six couples have related having a similar experience in the Joseph Kenny room, the one in which my wife and I stayed. Typically, he says, the wife will wake up and hear someone walk-ing around in the room, and assume it is her husband—until she notices he is still in bed with her. The husband, on the other hand, will dream about a woman dressed as a Civil War-era nurse who comes into the room, goes through it as if making her rounds, and then departs.

"And never before have we ever published this on our Web site [or] done any interviews or anything about it. So, it's not like they've read it somewhere and brought those stories with them." His interview for this book, Jerry says, is the first time he has discussed the hauntings at the 1848 Island Manor House for the record.

The third ghost, which appears to be that of a middle-aged servant, is the least obtrusive of the three, Jerry says, but has still been noticed by both him and a number of guests. Women in particular, he says, have heard a voice calling to them from the uppermost room at the front of the Kenny house, but have been unable to make out the words that are apparently being spoken to them.

Other local residents have also confirmed that they believe ghosts are present in the 1848 Island Manor House. Most notable is artist Katherine Kiss, owner of the nearby Guinevere's boutique, who says she is sensitive to the presence of spirits and has also confirmed that the inn is home to at least three ghosts. (Katherine has also noticed ghosts in at least one other house in Chincoteague, and says that the town hosts a relatively high number of them by virtue of the fact that it is such an old community.)

Jerry says he has tried to research a connection between these ghosts and the properties that comprise the inn and has spoken with previous owners about it but has not been able to;

A mischievous little girl purportedly haunts the 1848 Island Manor House and has been credited with moving around the pieces of the chess board in this sunroom.

the nurse is perhaps the most obvious and could certainly have been one of the women that tended wounded soldiers during the war. But why she and the others have remained in the house is by no means clear.

One theory is that they are happy at the inn and, while they may eventually resolve whatever issues have kept them upon the material plane and eventually move on or fade away, for the time being they are relatively content where they are.

And the fact that no connection can be proven between the ghosts and the history of the house is not necessarily significant, Katherine says. They might have been inadvertently brought in over the years by a visitor to the site and simply remained there because it felt right to them.

I did not experience any dreams of a Civil War nurse while at the inn (although I will admit that the active and melodic wind chimes in the courtyard outside my window did give my sleep a somewhat otherworldly quality). Nor did my wife and I experience anything indicative of a supernatural presence (despite her repeated and vocal assertions of hope that we would). If what Jerry says about the personalities of the ghosts living in his establishment is true, however, then encountering evidence of their presence would have only enhanced an already enjoyable visit.

CHAPTER 15

Colonial Williamsburg
WILLIAMSBURG

Spirits that have been dormant for centuries can be awakened by a flurry of activity and sounds. In the 1920s and 1930s, a major restoration project found the village of Williamsburg undergoing complete re-creation. It is possible that the constant pounding of hammers and the digging by archaeologists may have jolted some of these spirits from their sleep.

—Jackie Eileen Behrend, *The Hauntings of Williamsburg, Yorktown, and Jamestown*

MANY TIMES OVER THE YEARS I have walked the darkened streets of Colonial Williamsburg late at night, often in an attempt to clear my head a bit after some party before turning in. Despite the fact that on any number of those occasions not a single other living human being was in sight, I often felt that I was not alone, and that other people were moving about me on the ancient byways of the sleeping town.

Colonial Williamsburg—one point of the "Historic Triangle" that also includes Jamestown and Yorktown—is the historic district of the modern city of Williamsburg and includes many of the buildings that were part of the capital of the British colony of Virginia from 1699 to 1780 (although its first structures were built as early as 1632). Located on the high point of the Virginia Peninsula about halfway between the James and York Rivers, the town was prominent both geographically and as a center of politics, education, and culture. It was named in honor of King William III of Great Britain.

After the Revolutionary War began, the capital was moved to Richmond, fifty-five miles to the west, for security reasons and never returned to Williamsburg, which thereafter slipped into relative obscurity for several decades. It regained some prominence during the Civil War, when Union and Confederate forces fought for control over the strategic area it commanded. It returned to a somewhat sleepy and increasingly marginalized existence for the following half-century or so, however, and the historic district began slowly to decay.

Then, in the early 20th century, millionaire John D. Rockefeller Jr., his wife, Abby, and the Reverend Dr. W.A.R. Goodwin began to champion the restoration of Williamsburg as a way to educate people and honor the patriots who participated in the struggle for American independence. Spurred by their efforts, renovation of the district began in 1926 and continued initially into the 1930s—and since then into the present—during which time existing buildings were restored as closely as possible to how they were thought to have looked during the 18th century. Many vanished Colonial-era structures were also reconstructed on their original sites. All signs of later improvements and buildings were removed.

Today, the historic area is run as a living history center that interprets life in Colonial America through dozens of authentic or accurately recreated buildings and exhibits. Most of the roughly five hundred buildings in the historic district are open to visitors—with the exception of several that serve as residences for Colonial Williamsburg personnel—and some eighty-eight of them are original.

In the nearly two decades I have lived in Virginia, I have visited Colonial Williamsburg at least seven times for a variety of reasons, including family vacations, research for my *Living History* magazine, and for an annual conference that I used to attend on behalf of yet another magazine. Other than a distinct feeling that this oldest city of Virginia intersects with the unseen world, I never saw anything that I would take as credible evidence for the presence of ghosts. Innumerable other people have, however, and it would be completely accurate to say that the population of ghosts purported to haunt the district far exceeds the number of living people who now dwell within it (most of whom are now researchers and historical interpreters affiliated with the Colonial Williamsburg Foundation that was initially endowed by Rockefeller).

My wife, brother, and I all spent a weekend at Williamsburg in the 1990s and stayed at a historic property called the Chiswell-Bucktrout House, one of the historic properties associated with the Williamsburg Inn (which had once served as accommodations for British Prime Minister Margaret Thatcher during a visit to her government's former colonial capital).

This two-story, nine-room house does, in fact, have a violent past, and its owner, mercurial military officer Colonel John Chiswell, was accused of murder in 1766. Freed on bail pending his trial, he was himself discovered dead before the court could determine his guilt or innocence. A number of ghost stories have been associated with this house over the years, and with the detached kitchen (now also used as lodgings), including tales of sleeping people being awakened by ghosts touching or talking to them. I recall sleeping rather heavily the weekend I spent there, however, during which I discovered the delights of fortified wine, a Colonial-era favorite.

Just a few blocks northeast of the Chiswell-Bucktrout House, at the east end of Duke of Gloucester Street, is the old capitol—the first such building in America—a large structure that has been carefully recreated and landscaped as closely as possible to its original 18th century appearance with the help of period descriptions and illustrations. George Washington, Thomas Jefferson, and Patrick Henry were among the famous members of the House of Burgesses who met there in its day. Fire destroyed it in 1747, after which it was rebuilt, falling into disrepair and eventually being abandoned after the state capital was moved to Richmond, and the building now standing on the site is a 1930s recreation of the 1705 building.

A number of ghost stories have been associated with this site, but while it is possible that some or even many of them are true, they generally seem more fanciful and have a less credible ring to me than many.

"Some Williamsburg inhabitants go so far as to say that on the stroke of midnight on every Fourth of July there is an assemblage of Revolutionary ghosts, with Patrick Henry at their head, who stand in front of the capitol and use the most reprehensible language," wrote William Oliver Stevens in his 1938 book *Old Williamsburg,* which sounds less like a ghost story than like someone complaining about a long-forgotten issue of the day they were upset about.

Just to the north of the capitol at the east end of Duke of Gloucester Street is the Public Records Office, a fire-resistant brick building constructed in 1748 after many documents were destroyed in the blaze at the Capitol the previous year. It eventually ended up serving many other purposes over the years, and by the turn of the 20th century was home to David Roland Jones, his wife, and their seven daughters. One of them, a myopic young woman named Edna, is said to have snuck out of the house one night for an assignation with a young man. While en route to her tryst, the weak-eyed girl, possibly distracted by ardor for her lover or fear of her father, stepped out in front of a speeding carriage—a common hazard upon the darkened streets of Colonial cities, no doubt—and was killed. Since then, witnesses have reported seeing her ghost peeking from around corners of the building; floating over the graves of the nearby family plot; or calling out to women, who look to her spectral but still-deficient eyes, to be her friends.

Moving westward along Duke of Gloucester Street a little ways will bring a visitor to the Raleigh Tavern, a venerable institution first established in 1717, razed by fire in 1859, and subsequently rebuilt in its original form in 1932. Named for Walter Raleigh, its rich history involves serving as a meeting place for Revolutionary agitators and being the location for the 1776 founding of the Phi Beta Kappa fraternity. While ale flowed, dice rolled, and high ideas were discussed inside the tavern, slaves and other commodities were sold outside on its steps.

Some of the oldest ghost stories for any site in Colonial Williamsburg are about this location and have been documented as far back as 1856, three years before the destruction of the original building. These stories are all fairly uniform and typically involve passersby who detect signs of revelry within the building, including music, singing, clinking of glasses, and the smell of tobacco smoke.

Continuing west to the north end of Duke of Gloucester Street, then north a little ways along the Palace Green brings a visitor to the Wythe House, one of the sites in Colonial Williamsburg with the greatest reputation for being haunted. Considered by many to be the most attractive house in the city, the two-story brick manor dates to the 1750s and was owned by George Wythe, a leader of the Revolutionary movement in Virginia, a delegate to the Continental Congress, and the state's first signer of the Declaration of Independence. It also served as George Washington's headquarters prior to the British siege of Yorktown; French General Rochambeau used it as his headquarters after victory at Yorktown; and Thomas Jefferson lived there in 1776 while a delegate to the Virginia General Assembly.

The ghost mentioned most often in the traditional cycle of tales about the Wythe House is that of Lady Ann Skipwith, a temperamental young woman who is said to have fled a ball at a nearby house in a tiff, losing a shoe before ending up at Wythe House, and somehow dying mysteriously there (although some authors contest this latter detail and claim she died later and somewhere else). Her ghost, seen stylishly clad in a cream satin dress or heard clomping along on her single shoe, has been reported many times over the years. Other ghosts reported by various witnesses and authorities include Wythe himself, apparently poisoned in Richmond by an avaricious nephew, and George Washington (although the latter are more likely to be of some other poor devil in powdered wig and frock coat, unimaginative witnesses or storytellers generally preferring to simply see the ubiquitous Washington than to ascertain the identities of more obscure or less interesting individuals). A number of other ghosts have been cited in the works of various authors and psychic researchers.

Walking across the Palace Green and westward again, this time on Nicholson Street, will quickly bring a visitor to the

Peyton Randolph House, originally built in 1715 and restored between 1938 and 1940. It is widely considered to be one of the most beautiful homes in the city and notable guests from the Revolutionary War era included Washington, Lafayette, and Rochambeau. Its owner at that time was Betty Randolph, widow of Peyton Randolph. After she died in 1782, the house was sold at auction.

Apparently, so were many of her slaves, including one named Eve. Betty is reputed to have treated this woman especially badly, and to have had her sold off as a deliberately cruel means of separating her from her family. As she was be carried off into bondage elsewhere, some stories say, the embittered Eve called down a curse upon the house and its inhabitants. A number of people are said to have killed themselves or died suddenly in the house over the ensuing decades, and some believe that Eve's curse might be responsible. Others—including Lafayette himself, who stayed in the house during an 1824 return visit to America—have reported feeling ghostly hands upon their shoulders, being shaken awake while asleep in bed, and hearing a constant muttering of ghostly voices.

Those are just some of the Colonial Williamsburg buildings reputed to be haunted in some way, and it would be an understatement to say that entire books could be written about the subject of locations inhabited by ghosts within the historic district.

It would not necessarily be accurate to assume, of course, that all the ghostly activity at Colonial Williamsburg has its roots in the 18th century or even the Civil War. Many generations of people have lived in the town during periods that, while they may have been less exciting from a historical perspective, were just as relevant to their participants. So, while the vision for the creators and custodians of Colonial Williamsburg is that it should reflect America's Revolutionary War history, it is a bit much to ask spirits to either manifest themselves or remain quiet based on the eras in which they lived. It bears mentioning, too, that not all local residents were pleased with the transformation of their town in the 1930s, and some of them protested it arduously. It is certainly easy to imagine such angst being carried into the afterlife, and the ghost bearing it becoming progressively agitated at being identified not just as someone else but, indeed, as an inhabitant of an era other than his own—and on the basis of aesthetics no less.

CHAPTER 16

Fort Monroe
HAMPTON

We passed through a range of low arches, descended, passed on, and descending again, arrived at a deep crypt, in which the foulness of the air caused our flambeaux rather to glow than flame.

—Edgar Allan Poe, "The Cask of Amontillado"

MY FIRST EXPOSURE to ghosts at Fort Monroe, the legendary "Gibraltar of Chesapeake Bay," occurred a decade ago, when I visited the post as a member of the U.S. Army Inspector General Agency. My purpose then was official, and, as was the convention, the local inspector general provided me with a tour of the post.

I have visited most, if not all, of the Army's posts in the
United States. Many, like Fort Meyer in Virginia or Fort Leaven-
worth in Kansas, are steeped in history. Others, like the Presidio
of Monterey, are remarkable for their setting. But none is like
Fort Monroe. It is truly the most unique post in the country. It
is not just the only Army fort surrounded by a moat, it is also the
one with the earliest history. In 1609, two years after the first
permanent English settlement was founded at Jamestown and
eleven years before the Mayflower landed at Plymouth Rock, a
fortification called Algernourne Fort was started on this very
site by a detachment from Jamestown. There have been fortifications of various sorts here ever since.

The present fort resulted from lessons learned in the War of
1812. In 1813, the British fleet made anchor in Hampton Roads
harbor, raided the village of Hampton, and in 1814 proceeded
up the Chesapeake Bay to burn the city of Washington, D.C. Not
wishing to ever again repeat this ignominy, Congress ordered
the construction of the present fort in 1819. It was virtually completed by 1834—and none other than Robert E. Lee, then a lieutenant, oversaw the final stages of construction. The quarters
that Lee resided in with his wife are much the same today as
they were then.

Fort Monroe was originally named Fortress Monroe, a desig-
nation that, while incorrect, was probably a result of biblical and
religious connotations (e.g., "a mighty fortress is our God"). By
definition, however, a fortress encloses a town, and Fort Monroe
does not. For that reason, the U.S. Secretary of War renamed the
post Fort Monroe in 1832, although the U.S. Postal Service did
not change the name on its records for more than a century—
not until 1941.

Fort Monroe, including its moat, occupies an area of sixty-
three acres. With an armament of nearly two hundred guns,
it dominated the channel into Hampton Roads and controlled

the sea approach to Washington by way of the Chesapeake Bay, much as the British fortifications at Gibraltar dominated access to the Mediterranean.

It was a beautiful spring day back in the late 1990s when the Fort Monroe IG and I set out on foot from his office. We walked toward the red-brick ramparts of the fort and crossed the causeway. As we emerged from the arched gateway of the main sally port, we stepped into another age—a gracious era of officers in tailored blue uniforms and hoop-skirted ladies. We strolled past stately antebellum residences, including the one where Lieutenant Robert E. Lee had once resided. Then we turned right onto Ruckman Road and proceeded past the narrow lane known as "Ghost Alley." My guide, however, did not comment on that, and I have no idea if he even knew of the nickname for that quiet sunlit alleyway that ran behind those elegant quarters.

Shortly, on our left, however, we came to what appeared to be a vacant house—that is to say, unoccupied family quarters. It was a wood-framed and wood-sided structure that appeared to date from the late 1800s or early 1900s. Unlike the other quarters we had passed, this one had a run-down and almost abandoned look.

"It's haunted," the IG said. "Nobody wants to live there, so the housing office just leaves it vacant."

He went on to tell me about what had spooked earlier residents. I listened, amused—skeptical, but with an open mind. He was, after-all, the inspector general. Unfortunately, I took no notes. That was not what I was there for. Now, of course, I wish I had recorded it all. I've tried in vain to recall the details of what he said to me, but I only retain a faint recollection of ghostly sightings, strange noises, and blinds that would not stay down—or maybe it was up.

But the basic memory never left me, and when I had the opportunity to return to Fort Monroe specifically for the purpose of researching the matter of ghosts, I took the task on eagerly in the hope of finally getting to the bottom of my recollections.

Having been an IG, and knowing "how things should be done," my first step was to contact the official voice of Fort Monroe, the Public Affairs Office. In what I have now seen, in retrospect, as a pattern, officialdom was not at all eager to discuss the subject. Whether they believed the topic to be frivolous, or whether they had something to hide, I cannot say. Suffice it to say, I obtained no satisfaction from the telephone call. I even brought up my previous visit, some ten years earlier as an IG, and what the local IG had told me. This elicited only nervous consternation, and a hasty, "I cannot comment on that." In short, my hopes of a productive interview with the Public Affairs Office were dashed. All that remained was to go to Fort Monroe and see what I could find out for myself.

I had done my research and knew that there were many ghost stories associated with the fort—not to mention the "moat monster" that a colonel had reported seeing swimming in the moat surrounding the fort. There were also a number of the stories set in the casemates and the museum that is now located there. This is where Confederate President Jefferson Davis had been imprisoned after the Civil War. It was also where America's arguably greatest writer of ghost stories, Edgar Allan Poe, had been stationed as a young soldier in the 1820s, when the fort was still under construction.

I believe, whatever one's purpose, that the Casemate Museum is the best place to start an exploration of Fort Monroe. It is the one place where a visitor still has access to the casemates. It is also where the cannons that guarded the approaches to the Chesapeake were situated. Moreover, the marvelous exhibits give the visitor an excellent introduction to Fort Monroe and what life would have been like there during the 19th century. There is, among the many exhibits, the cell in which Jefferson

Davis was so cruelly imprisoned by a vengeful nation. It is also here that his ghost is reported to return, revisiting the site of his torment and humiliation in conditions that surely hastened his passing. (This is not where Jefferson Davis actually died, although some sources allege otherwise.)

It only took a single glance down the range of low brick arches that supported the ceiling of the casemates to grasp the inspiration for the story that Sergeant Poe wrote while stationed here, "The Cask of Amontillado." Fort Monroe in those days, being still under construction, must have been strewn with piles of bricks and sacks of mortar as the masons went about their decade-and-a-half task. And if that were not enough, there was also a story in circulation of a soldier who had been bricked up behind one of those walls. But one cannot help but wonder if there was even more than that. Fort Monroe and, indeed, the whole Virginia coast, as I was to learn, is steeped in ghosts and supernatural occurrences. Almost everybody I met had a ghost story—or, to be more precise, almost everybody who wasn't a public affairs officer. A tour guide at the nearby Fort Story assured me that the Virginia coast is the most haunted locale in the United States. One can only wonder what influence serving in such a place had on the young and still-impressionable Poe.

The tour of the Casemate Museum ends in the bookstore. There I heard my first account of a ghostly sighting. Some weeks earlier, parents, visiting the bookstore after their tour, reported what their young daughter had told them. She had been viewing one of the historical exhibits when something inexplicable occurred. It was an artillery exhibit, with several life-sized manikins in post-Civil War uniforms in the process of servicing an artillery piece. The little girl reported that one of the life-sized manikins had turned to her and had warned her to cover her ears as they prepared to fire their cannon.

I talked to a number of other employees who also had stories to tell. They requested, however, that I not reveal their identities. Suffice it to say, they were well-placed to receive the accounts of visitors to the post and to the museum. I must admit, although I am a skeptic on the issue of ghosts, the stories had an aura of credibility. They were received directly from those involved and reported to me by an official who was also a skeptic. There is not space to recount them all here. The two that follow I found not only to be interesting and credible, but I also could not find them published anywhere else.

One story occurred several years earlier but had made a lasting impression on my reporter, an Army wife, still shaking from her experience. She had been standing in the window of her quarters, which were to the left of the former post commander's house known as Quarters One (where the ghost of Abraham Lincoln is said to make an occasional appearance). She was watching an interview with Boy George conducted by Barbara Walters, taking place on the grounds below. All of a sudden, the table behind her rose up and flew into the fireplace as the lamp that was on it hurtled to the other side of the room. Between the table and the fireplace was the family dog, who was so startled that he scratched the floor so deeply that the post engineers were never able to buff the marks out.

Another story involved a military family that that had just moved into the old, now-demolished pre-World War II white, framed quarters locally known as "white elephants." The wife was unpacking the boxes containing their household goods and, each time she cut open a box, she would set the knife on the refrigerator. But every time she went to reach for it, it had moved to another location. Finally, in frustration, she shouted. "Get out of my house and don't come back!"

That seemed to solve the problem—but when the family was moving out, there was another occurrence, which maybe held the explanation for the strange events that had occurred when they had first moved in. All their possessions had been packed up, and the family was standing in front of the quarters waiting for transportation when their young son went back into the house to get a drink of water. He stepped into the kitchen and saw another little boy, but this one was wearing a long white smock, as was the fashion in the 19th century. Evidently, this boy was the prankster who had kept moving the knife. Having been ordered away, he waited patiently until the family had departed before returning to what may well have been his home. Now that this house has been torn down, one can only wonder what refuge that boy has since found.

There are also a number of stories at Fort Monroe that involve family pets, usually cats. Sometimes a cat is seen in the quarters of a family that doesn't own one. In other cases, the cat mysteriously leaves and enters closed rooms. What is interesting is that none of the accounts ever link these pet stories to what I found to be one of the most unique features of Fort Monroe—the pet cemetery.

Since at least the 1930s, military families have used this part of Fort Monroe as a pet cemetery.

The ramparts of the fort are faced with red brick on the moat side, but on the inside they are composed of packed earth and rise approximately forty feet above the inside level of the fort. There were once gun emplacements here, and their iron tracks are still visible. All along this earthen embankment, interspersed between the iron tracks, are the graves of the family pets of the soldiers once stationed here. When this custom started I have no idea. The earliest grave I could find was from 1936. Most are either conventional granite headstones or homemade concrete slabs. There were also some of less durable material, such as wooden crosses, many of which had undoubtedly deteriorated. One can only wonder if at the root of some of the stories is the ghost of a beloved family pet vainly searching the family quarters for masters who, subject to military orders, have long since moved on to other assignments.

I should also mention the small but very excellent bookstore located in the casemate. It carries a number of books dealing with the subject of ghosts at Fort Monroe and the surrounding area. These included two coauthored by Jane Polonsky, the wife of a retired Army colonel who had once served on the post.

Among the stories is the one about the so-called "White Lady." Some say her name was Camille Kirtz, although the Fort Monroe historian told me there is no record of a woman with that name ever having lived at the fort. Nevertheless, this is Fort Monroe's oldest documented ghost story. Legend has it that it is because of Camille that Mathew's Lane has been called "Ghost Alley" since at least 1885. The story that has drifted down over the years is that it was here, in the alley, that this beautiful young woman would meet her lover, a dashing young officer (some accounts have him a French officer) with flowing mustaches and a flair for the ladies. Unfortunately for the lovers, Camille was married—so their trysts had to take place not only after darkness had fallen, but also only when Captain Kirtz was away. From the alley, the lovers would then enter her quarters by the stable entrance. As luck would have it, the husband returned unexpectedly one night to find the pair in his bed. Enraged, he snatched up a pistol and shot his wife. The young officer made his escape, and the "White Lady" is still sometimes seen searching for him at the stable entrances on Ghost Alley.

So what about the "haunted" house that the IG had shown me on my first visit to Fort Monroe a decade ago? It is still there on Ruckman Road and it is still vacant. My current source, however—who had regaled me with so many stories of ghosts and mysterious happenings—assured me that he had never heard of any ghostly sightings associated with this property. It had been condemned, he said, by the post engineers because of structural issues, not supernatural ones.

I have no reason to doubt the truthfulness of that assertion. Rather, I suspect that the IG, having heard many ghost stories associated with the post—to include stories of quarters that families had refused to live in (documented in Jane Polonsky's books)—had leapt to a logical, but ultimately incorrect, conclusion. Many quarters at Fort Monroe are haunted, but not all of them are, and there are still structural and maintenance issues whose causes are solely of this plane.

MOUNTAIN

VIRGINIA: MOUNTAIN AREA

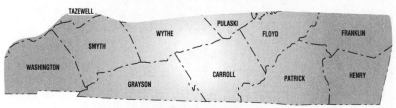

North Carolina

Abingdon
 Barter Theater

Fancy Gap
 Devil's Den

Hillsville
 Carroll County Courthouse

Lee, Scott, Washington, Grayson,Carroll, and Patrick Counties
 US Route 58

Marion
 Octagon House

CHAPTER 17

Barter Theatre
ABINGDON

To-morrow, and to-morrow, and to-morrow,
Creeps in this petty pace from day to day
To the last syllable of recorded time,
And all our yesterdays have lighted fools
The way to dusty death. Out, out, brief candle!
Life's but a walking shadow, a poor player
That struts and frets his hour upon the stage
And then is heard no more.

—William Shakespeare, *Macbeth*, Act 5, Scene 5

IN 1933, at the height of the Great Depression, an actor named Robert Porterfield, along with many of his colleagues, was out of work and hungry in New York City. He decided to return to his home region of southwestern Virginia, where food was still plentiful. Once there, he launched an innovative enterprise that both brought entertainment to the people of the isolated mountainous region and allowed himself and his friends to survive in their chosen vocation. It was to become the great work of his life—and, some people believe, has continued beyond it.

"With vegetables you cannot sell, you can buy a good laugh," was the slogan of the theatre when it opened June 10, 1933. Price of admission to the aptly named Barter Theatre was thirty-five cents or the equivalent in produce, and the concept of trading "ham for Hamlet" caught on quickly with the local people (who, presumably, were not induced to laugh at the gloomy Dane despite the various catch phrases of the institution). "At the end of the first season," according to the theatre's published history, "the Barter Company cleared $4.35 in cash, two barrels of jelly, and enjoyed a collective weight gain of over three hundred pounds."

Porterfield established his theatre in a building that had originally been constructed in 1831 as a Presbyterian church. Just six years later, it was acquired by the "Sons of Temperance," an anti-drinking organization that used it for various events in the years before, during, and after the Civil War, during which the building was caught up in some of the fighting that swept through the town of Abingdon. And, in the decade after the war, while it was still known as "Temperance Hall," it was used on January 14, 1876, for its first theatrical performance, a production of *The Virginian.*

In 1890, the town of Abingdon acquired the building from the Sons of Temperance and converted it into a town hall, jail house, and fire station. One of the improvements made during this era was the addition of a fire siren on the roof of the building, which remained there even after it became a theatre and would sometimes sound during its performances. When this would happen, the actors on stage would freeze in place until it had stopped and then would resume their performance where it had been interrupted (a tradition that continued for more than six decades, until 1994, when the fire department shifted over to a new system for alerting firefighters).

Porterfield spared no effort to make the luxurious, five-hundred-seat Barter Theatre a success in the four decades that he directed it. One of the stories most often told about his dedication involves the old Empire Theatre in New York City, which had been built in 1875 and in 1953 was slated to be demolished and replaced with an office building. Porterfield obtained permission to remove all that he could from the doomed theatre but only had one weekend in which to do so, so he organized a crew of volunteers, pulled everything he could out of the Empire, and then had it loaded on trucks and shipped nearly six hundred miles overland to Abingdon.

All told, Porterfield managed to salvage about $75,000 worth of furnishings and equipment, including seats, carpeting, paintings in large gold frames, red wall tapestries, and a lighting system designed and installed by Thomas Edison that remained in use at the Barter through the mid-1970s. Most of the Empire elements were removed in 1995, when the Barter was completely renovated. Those remaining to this day include four sculptures holding lighting fixtures and a number of portraits, among them those of thespians Dennis King (in the Empire's production of *The Three Musketeers*), Maude Adams (as Peter Pan), and Katherine Cornell.

In 1961, Porterfield acquired another historic property, across the street from the Barter Theatre, and converted into a second, smaller stage that is used for more avant-garde performances.

It began its existence in 1829 as a Methodist church and subsequently served as part of the Stonewall Jackson Female Institute, as a chapter house, and by Martha Washington College, first as a gymnasium and then as a storage area. The Barter Theatre has made significant improvements to the 167-seat theatre a number of times over the years, including in 1973; again in 1985, with the addition of a lobby and a memorial garden; and in 2003, with improved seating and a café. Additional refinements were made in 2004.

Barter Theatre has enjoyed a great deal of success, and many luminaries of the stage and screen have been associated with it over the years. Playwrights who accepted Virginia ham as payment for royalties, for example, included Noel Coward, Tennessee Williams, and Thornton Wilder (vegetarian George Bernard Shaw having instead bartered the rights to his plays for spinach). Actors who walked upon its stage before achieving fame included Ned Beatty, Ernest Borgnine, James Burrows (creator of *Cheers*), Gary Collins, Barry Corbin, Hume Cronyn, Frances Fisher, Larry Linville, Patricia Neal, Gregory Peck, Kevin Spacey, and Jim Varney. And in 1946, the Barter was designated "the State Theatre of Virginia."

Barter Theatre has also enjoyed recognition beyond its home region, and, in a tradition of touring that dates to the year of its founding, its troupe gives visiting performances throughout the states of Virginia, Alabama, Florida, Georgia, Kentucky, Maryland, Ohio, North Carolina, South Carolina, Tennessee, and West Virginia. It even gave its first international performance in 1949, when part of the Barter company took a production of *Hamlet* to Denmark.

Today, Barter Theatre has more than 140,000 annual patrons and a staff that includes 135 fulltime employees and as many as an additional 145 seasonal ones. And beyond its two stages, the Barter Theatre today also has administrative offices, rehearsal

halls, and dormitories set up in an additional half-dozen buildings throughout Abingdon.

By the time Robert Porterfield died in 1971 at the age of sixty-
five, he had clearly created through his passion and dedication a
lasting legacy that has continued to grow. There are suggestions
from some, however, that he never left it behind and that his
spirit not only inhabits the theatre but that it is not alone.

"It hasn't happened recently, but there used to be a certain
seat in the theatre that he always used to sit in, and people would
swear that they would see him sitting there in that white sweater
he was known for, watching rehearsals and plays years after he
had died," Peter Yonka, director of marketing for the theatre,
told my wife and me when we visited the theater in May 2008.
Yonka himself used to be an actor with the theatre and left it for
some time before returning in his current capacity (which still
includes the opportunity to act, as he was rehearsing for the role
of Che in *Evita* during our visit).

"Porterfield is larger than life," Yonka said, and noted that
organizations often don't survive long after their driving forces
disappear but that this has most assuredly not been the case
with the Barter. "He's still a positive presence here [and] people
claim to have seen him. It's been awhile, though."

Indeed, while Yonka has personally spoken with actors who
say they have seen Porterfield in the Barter Theatre in the years
since his death, none claim that this has happened recently—
perhaps not since the major renovations to the theatre in the
mid-1990s.

"There have been paranormal investigators that have come
and stayed overnight at the Barter," Yonka said, indicating the
continuing interest of ghosthunters, even in the possible absence
of a reciprocal sentiment from the theatre's main ghost. It may
be that he is not the only one to have ever haunted the Barter
Theatre, however, and Yonka told us that a number of others

have been seen or sensed by people in the institution's various buildings over the years.

In the basement of the main theatre building, for example, the boiler room underneath the stage once had a tunnel leading from it to the Martha Washington Inn across the street. This room is supposed to be the site of several brutal killings during the Civil War, and a disquieting sense that the spirits of the dead men are still present has led actors and stage crew—especially those who have had to go into it by themselves or at night—to dub it "the Scary Room."

"Two Confederate soldiers were running guns between what is now the Barter Theatre and the Martha Washington Inn, a girls' school that was used as a hospital during the war," Yonka said. "They were caught by Union soldiers who shot and killed them in the tunnel. They were buried there when the tunnel collapsed."

Since then, a number of people have sensed a very angry presence in the room and the feeling that they were not welcome there. Some have even heard a voice telling them to "Get out!" Yonka said. It is right next to the costume room, he added, and people do not like to linger there by themselves after shows and generally take care of what they need to as soon as possible so that they can leave.

Yonka was both kind and brave enough to take us down to the Scary Room during our visit, and, even with three of us there during the early evening, it was definitely creepy. One thing that enhanced this feeling, of course, was the presence of a low metal door that served no other function than to cover the opening to the now-filled-in tunnel that had once been there. Rather than simply brick this up, someone had had the almost perverse forethought to put a door on it, so that no one could ever conveniently forget it was there. We did not experience anything paranormal during our visit to the theater, but if we had,

Door leading to the filled-in tunnel in the Scary Room

I suspect it would have occurred here. During our visit to the Barter Theatre, Diane and I also attended the final production for the current run of *Look on the Sunny Side,* which told the story of the Carter family, a local clan of musicians that played a major role in the early years of country music and into which Johnny Cash married.

Throughout the performance, I kept glancing toward the spot where we were told that Porterfield used to be seen, at the front of the theater and to the left of the stage, near where rows of elevated boxes used to be. Those were removed during the major renovations in 1995, and maybe, I reflected, that was why

Porterfield was no longer seen sitting in the theatre during performances. Sitting in a private box over the stage, after all, has a certain elegance, even for a ghost, but just hovering in the air where a box used to be could be kind of horrifying.

Perhaps a desire to keep from upstaging his own actors and spoiling their performances was part of the reason Porterfield had not been spotted for so long in his familiar spot. And, perhaps too, I thought, his desire to be a continuing part of the great thing he had created might not have been as great as his sense that the show must go on, with or without him.

CHAPTER 18

Carroll County Courthouse
HILLSVILLE

In the small courthouse at Hillsville, Virginia, on the morning of March 14, 1912, occurred the tragedy that sent my brother, Floyd Allen, and his son, Claude, to their deaths in the electric chair, and caused me, following my arrest six months later, to be sentenced to thirty-five years in prison.

—J. Sidna Allen, *Memoirs of J. Sidna Allen*

DESPITE THE FACT that it happened nearly a century ago, the defining episode in the history of Hillsville seems to be the shooting at the Carroll County Courthouse. People in Carroll County still debate the specifics of the deadly skirmish to this day, with particular emphasis being placed on such things as analysis of who fired first—the Allens and their kin or the officers of the court.

To an outsider with no emotional investment in the debate, the facts pretty much speak for themselves: Floyd Allen and a number of his relatives came to court with firearms hidden on their persons; when Floyd was sentenced to a year in jail he declared that he was not going; at least fifty-seven shots were fired over the next two minutes; and when the smoke cleared five people were dead—none of them members of the Allen clan—and seventeen were wounded. Suggestions that the sheriff and clerk of the court decided to publicly assassinate Floyd and his relatives are, on their face, absurd and a bit grotesque. But, as noted, people in Carroll County are even now still divided over this issue. And maybe that is part of the reason why, some believe, the spirits of those slain in the courthouse can still sometimes be sensed within it.

Many of the ghostly phenomena that have been reported in the Carroll County Courthouse in the decades since the shooting took place have, significantly, occurred on the anniversary of the incident. Most of those involve the sound of a spectral gavel banging down again and again, year after year, in commemoration of the judgment leveled against the man who would have flouted the law of the land.

Interestingly, the other things that people most commonly report seeing correspond eerily to the two camps of sentiment in the ongoing debate over what really happened in March 1912.

On the one hand, passersby and those who have found themselves alone in the courthouse for whatever reasons have reported seeing spectral images of the various people shot and killed in the courthouse massacre. Almost invariably, such witnesses have been able to recognize which of the victims they were seeing, whether through some phantasmal iconography—

e.g., the one sitting behind the bench would obviously be the judge—or some intuitive sense.

On the other hand, people have seen the ghostly images of the various members of the Allen clan who participated in the shooting; none of them died in the shooting, of course, but all are dead now, so the case could certainly be made that any of them is now a ghost. In most cases, these apparitions have assumed postures suggestive of their fates (e.g., clad in the prison garb that they all eventually wore as a consequence of their participation in the events at the courthouse).

Very few people, if any, who have reported such incidents have reported both sorts. People are susceptible, it seems, to seeing one sort or the other when it comes these phenomena.

Whether any of these stories have any veracity, or whether they are simply devices for promoting one version of the events that occurred at the Carroll County Courthouse or another, is certainly not obvious to an outsider. It may very well be that both sets of stories are equally true and that some people are just more susceptible to perceiving one group of phenomena over the other.

Carroll County's history predates the incident for which it is most famous by a couple of centuries. A few families had settled in the area by the 1750s, and more followed when a number of roads into the region were built in the following decade—one of the first corresponding to what is now Main Street in Hillsville. About one hundred households existed in the region by the time of the Revolutionary War. Lead mining was the first industry in the area, dating to the time of its first settlement, but farming remained the mainstay of the economy until the 1980s, when manufacturing, government, and retailing became its biggest segments.

"Nearly every family owned its own piece of ground and was beholden to no man for it," wrote local historian John P. Alderman. "All were proud and fiercely independent." His words, taken in the context of the famous incident, assume a meaning they otherwise might not.

Quakers settled in the area in the early 19th century and at one point made up about a third of the population. After a few decades, however, they moved on to points north and west—taking with them, one might note, their pacifist ways.

Indeed, when the Civil War began, the county was home to 884 white males, ages 17 to 34—out of a total population of 8,012—and some 600 of them volunteered for military service under the Confederacy within six months. Stubbornness, a sense of adventure, and loyalty to Virginia, Alderman says, were the main motivations (slavery not being an issue to them, there being only 261 slaves in the entire county at the time).

Much has been written about the courthouse shooting, especially in the days, weeks, and months following it. In many of the contemporary newspaper accounts, the Allens and their kin were depicted as barbaric hillbillies, while in the writings of their apologists they are characterized as people who, despite being the salt of the earth, were inexplicably persecuted by enemies and sorely misunderstood by the public.

The truth, as always, would seem to be somewhere in between. What is known for sure is that Floyd Allen had a reputation as a mean-spirited bully who had a practice of intimidating his neighbors and threatening to kill them. In 1904, Floyd had nonfatally shot a man for buying a piece of land that he himself wanted. He was fined a mere $100 for this attack after threatening to kill the judge and jurors if he was convicted and sent to jail. So, the ongoing debate aside, it would seem to the dispassionate observer that what happened when Floyd ended up in court again eight years later was something he had made a practice of threatening to do.

Like the shooting itself, the events that led to Floyd Allen being in the courtroom the day of the shooting are still hotly debated (and, while somewhat sordid, are much less interesting than is warranted by the amount of attention they have received). A short version is that when two of his nephews, Wesley and Sidna Edwards, were arrested the previous year for brawling outside a church over a girl, Floyd rescued them from the sheriff and his deputy while they were being transported to jail. Accordingly, he was charged with "Illegal Rescue of Prisoners" and, after several continuances, had a trial date set for March 12, 1912.

He was convicted pretty quickly by a jury of his peers and sentenced by Judge Thornton L. Massie to a year in jail and a $1,000 fine.

"Gentlemen," Floyd Allen announced as the judge finished speaking. "I just ain't a goin.'" And then all hell broke loose.

Ultimately, Floyd Allen did go. Shot in the ensuing altercation and too wounded to flee, he went to jail, even as he declared he would not. And a year later, on March 28, 1914, he went to the electric chair, followed eleven minutes later by his son Claud. Three of his relatives, including his nephews Friel Allen and Wesley Edwards and his brother J. Sidna Allen, were sentenced to prison terms ranging from eighteen to thirty-five years.

In May 2008, my wife and I visited Hillsville and a number of sites associated with the courthouse shooting in an attempt to piece together as well as we could what had happened at the site and what the lasting effects of it might be.

Our first stop had been the day before we reached Hillsville, in nearby Galax, where we had visited Harmon's Outlet, a Western store that operates a museum of local history in a large back room. We learned a bit about the shooting there and picked up the book recommended by the staff, the *Memoirs of J. Sidna Allen: A True Narrative of What Really Happened at Hillsville, Virginia.* We later learned that the owner of the store is a member of the pro-Allen camp in the ongoing debate about the shooting and, as we started to read through the book, immediately learned it was a rather smug apologia.

"... a pistol cracked loudly. The sound indicated that the shot had been fired in the southeast corner of the room. Looking in that direction, I saw flashing guns in the hands of Dexter Goad, clerk of the court, and Lew Webb, the sheriff. Their weapons, I thought, were pointed directly at Floyd Allen and apparently they were attempting to kill him," Allen writes. "Snatching out my revolver I began firing at Goad, for by this time he was popping away at me."

If the clerk and sheriff had attempted to summarily execute Floyd Allen in a courtroom filled with some three hundred people, their dastardly plan backfired on them disastrously. Those killed included Webb, presiding Judge Thornton L. Massie, Commonwealth's Attorney William Foster, juror Augustus Fowler, and spectator Betty Ayers. Goad was among the many wounded.

We moved on to our second stop, Devil's Den, later the same day. A cluster of irregular caves at the bottom of a steep, wooded mountainside, it served as a hideout for a couple of the Allen clan gunmen in the weeks after the shooting. Our investigation confirmed to my complete satisfaction that it was actually haunted, but the presence of ghosts in it probably has nothing to do with the gun fight at the Carroll County Courthouse, as none of the shooters died—or are known to have killed anyone else— at the site. (It was a significant enough site to me, however, to devote a separate chapter to it in this section.)

Our venture into Devil's Den accomplished, we moved up the Blue Ridge Parkway a little ways to the Volunteer Gap Inn, where we spent the night. While we were there, we chatted with proprietors Ron and Deena McKinney. Ron told us about the local area and what he knew about the Carroll County Courthouse shooting, and filled in the gaps in our knowledge a little bit. Ron and I also compared notes about our respective experiences at Devil's Den, which he had visited the month before and found to be pretty creepy as well.

The next morning we hit the road and headed north toward the third stop on our journey. A few miles outside of Hillsville, we came to the home of J. Sidna Allen, who prior to the shooting had been a prosperous merchant and property owner and had had the Victorian mansion built shortly before the incidents to which he was party. Floyd Allen spent the night before the final day of his trial here, and many believe that it was here the two brothers formulated their plan for what would occur the following day.

Open to visitors on an irregular basis, the house is widely considered in the local neighborhood to be haunted. No one was there to show people around when we arrived, and the place was locked up. However, I walked around it anyway and peeked

The approach to the historic but crumbling and uncared-for J. Sidna Allen house, believed by many to be haunted by the ghost of its embittered former owner

through the shuttered windows to see what I could, while Diane kept an eye on the car. Whether the house was haunted or not I couldn't tell, but it certainly was creepy. The once-beautiful home was now neglected and crumbling from a lack of care, and inside its unfurnished rooms I could see little piles of debris scattered about.

Circling around the property, I passed by the back of the house and a number of outbuildings, and saw the same sort of neglect. On a rational level, I knew my apprehension that someone with a leather mask and a chainsaw would come running out at me from one of several half-closed doors was a product of the kinds of movies I watched, but I still felt kind of nervous and didn't linger. Returning to the car, I continued on the last few miles into Hillsville and the Carroll County Courthouse.

We visited the historic courthouse on a Sunday, when it is normally closed. I had made several calls to the numbers given for it and the museum the week before we made our trip to southwestern Virginia in an attempt to arrange a tour or interview, but no one bothered to return our calls. Sometimes, declaring oneself a ghosthunter makes people decide they don't need to respond, and sometimes they just aren't very courteous or professional to start with, and we had no way of knowing what the case was here.

Getting inside certainly would have been a plus, but even if we had spent another night in the area it would not have done any good, as the courthouse and museum were also closed on Mondays (not to mention, it was also Memorial Day). That was disappointing, as a firsthand examination of the courtroom would have been key to our assessment of whether or not it was haunted. And the museum was supposed to feature a number of relevant exhibits, including a number of pieces of furniture crafted by J. Sidna Allen while he was in the state penitentiary.

That left us with access only to the exterior of the building.

A largely neoclassical structure completed in 1874, it combines elements of various traditional courthouse forms, including an arcaded Doric portico in front of an arcaded ground floor and flanking wings, and is topped with an octagonal pinnacled cupola. In front of it is the Confederate war memorial that the Allens had used as cover while making a fighting withdrawal from the courthouse.

As I walked around the courthouse taking pictures, however, I was fortunate enough to discover that the Carroll County Chamber of Commerce was open that day and that its offices— also located in the basement of the courthouse—were manned by the chamber's executive director, Roger Hawthorne. I quickly went back to the car and rousted Diane, who had opted to wait for me there while I took pictures.

Hawthorne chatted with us for awhile about the courthouse and the shooting, and then very graciously showed us around the outside of it a little bit, pointing out some places where bullet holes from the 1912 shootout had been left in stairs leading up to the main entrance.

We did not see any signs of ghosts while we were in Hillsville, but I suspect there is a pretty good chance some were there. There was a measure of justice, after all, and Floyd Allen did ultimately pay for his crimes with his life, as did his son. And three others served time in prison for their part in the lawless act.

And yet the ghosts of the Carroll County Courthouse are not quiet. Possibly it is because after he had served a mere eleven years of his sentence, J. Sidna Allen had his sentence commuted when he was pardoned by the governor of Virginia. Maybe it is because people in and around Hillsville still besmirch the names of the dead and charge them with the crimes that led to their deaths. Perhaps it is because they continue to hope into death that there will ultimately be justice for the acts that ended their lives.

CHAPTER 19

Devil's Den
FANCY GAP

Dipping into the surrounding thorny woods, you find the Devil's Den, a cave carved inside the Blue Ridge with a name inspired by mystery, legend, and a network of seemingly endless channels. A folk tale says a man once spent a week inside this fault cave and came out three miles down the mountain. Exactly where the cave goes, it seems, is unknown.

—Joe Tennis, *Southwest Virginia Crossroads*

ON THE SUNDAY BEFORE MEMORIAL DAY in 2008, my wife and I spent a couple of hours at the Devil's Den Nature Preserve, a 240-acre park located at the eastern edge of the Blue

Ridge Escarpment, overlooking the foothills of North Carolina. It is right outside of Fancy Gap and just a few miles from the nearest entrance to the scenic Blue Ridge Parkway. That it warrants investigation far beyond what we were equipped to do during our short visit is an understatement.

What originally led us to the Devil's Den was a list of "Ghostly Haunts in Virginia" posted on the official tourism Web site of the Commonwealth of Virginia. "Huge rocks mark the entrance to the Devil's Den," the Web page says, "a cave that played a role in local history in association with the infamous 1912 Carroll County Courthouse shooting." This Web site cites but a single reference, the *National Register of Haunted Locations,* and implies that it is the source for the information on the "Virginia is for Lovers" Web site.

Beyond that single reference, however, source material on Devil's Den proved very difficult to find, as did any actual ghost stories about it. The *National Register of Haunted Locations*—a publication of Dale Kaczmarek's Ghost Research Society— seemed like a good first place to start, but there were no references in it to the site. Likewise, Internet searches, perusals through books of ghost stories written as early as the 1930s, even explorations through old histories of Carroll County, where it is located, revealed very little. Presumably, there is something more published about Devil's Den than what I was able to find, but it is not easy to locate.

Other bits of information I was able to obtain prior to our visit included that J. Sidna Allen, one of the men who participated in the lethal gun battle at the nearby Carroll County Courthouse in 1912, fled into the hills following the attack and apparently took refuge at Devil's Den for some time (likely a factor in it becoming a tourist attraction in the 1920s). It seems that the place had a history of being used as a hiding place for as long as anyone could remember and that it had very possibly sheltered escaped slaves as a stop on the Underground Railroad.

Once at the park, we were able to get a little more information from a sign at its entrance off Cemetery Road. It was the sort of charming information I usually found best to keep to myself, my wife generally finding it much less amusing than I do.

"The Devil's Den Cave is within the preserve and accessed by a strenuous path," the sign said in part. "Some areas are very DANGEROUS. Along the trail to the cave are cliffs and rocky ledges, which are not visible below your feet. Watch where you step, as a fall from these areas would result in SERIOUS INJURY or DEATH. ... Wild animals, including bears, are in the area. Do not try to feed or taunt them." The surrounding area would have been even wilder in centuries past, and it is little wonder that fugitive slaves and outlaws—those who could resist the urge to taunt the local dangerous wildlife, in any event—figured they could obtain a certain amount of sanctuary there.

We drove through the entryway and past the fenced Morris family cemetery on the left. A number of cars were parked just beyond it, and it was not immediately obvious to us that this was the parking area for the preserve, and we continued on to a dead-end near some utility infrastructure before we realized our mistake. (Gas prices aside, I will never regret using an SUV for expeditions like this.) Our mistake did provide us with a view into a wooded ravine containing an old house, evidently the Robert S. Harris Farmstead, a late-19th-century dwelling that is currently being renovated for use as a future exhibit at the park (and, based on its appearance alone, is almost certainly haunted).

Diane and I parked in the grassy field alongside a number of other vehicles, exchanged pleasantries with some of the other people milling about, and tried to obtain any additional information we could about the site. Some kids told us they had spotted several snakes while hiking on the trail that disappeared into the nearby wood line—something we were not too happy to hear.

A sign at the head of the trail indicated it led a mere 0.46 miles to the Devil's Den. As we followed it into the wood line, it began to descend immediately through thick vegetation. To our right, the hill sloped back up toward the meadow where we had started. To the left, it tumbled away into a rocky, forested ravine. Stands of pine alternated with groves of leafy trees of various sorts, and thick clumps of mountain laurel clung to a number of dark, rocky outcroppings. The one thing that moderated the wildness of the place was the presence of periodic benches, perhaps a half dozen of them, placed at the side of the trail. These seemed a bit extraneous for such a short trail, and we did not avail ourselves of them (their utility became apparent on the steep walk back, however, when we made use of every one of them).

After perhaps a quarter mile the trail became steeper and

Path leading to Devil's Den

rougher, and, maybe a quarter mile after that, it split. We went to the left, following some crude blazes on the trees, and we could hear a group of four following a ways behind us head noisily off to the right.

The way only got worse as we progressed and lost most of its claim to being called a trail. To our right, it fell away into a wooded gorge, a fall into which would certainly have resulted in some injury. On our left, it wound around the edge of the hill, curving out of sight so that we had no sense of what was just ahead of us.

"Are you sure we're going in the right direction?" Diane asked me a little bit irritably.

"How," I asked, turning to give her a hand over a particularly rough spot, "could I possibly be *sure* we're going in the right direction? I've never been here before. But I obviously *think* we're going in the right direction or else I wouldn't be going this way." Somewhere off in the direction of the other trail, we could hear the little boy in the group that had gone that way yelling that he could see the cave.

Something about his tone, however, suggested he was lying, and I continued leading us in the direction we had chosen. And, almost immediately, we emerged onto the entryway of the Devil's Den. Our sense was that the distance was probably one-and-a-half times as far as the sign had indicated, and that the 0.46 miles was a straight-line map measurement that did not take into account the slope of the trail.

Devil's Den is impressive but in no way inviting. Its entryway consists of several huge slabs of rock, rising as much as fifty feet above the approach and pitched over on each other in such a way as to produce a covered area over a forty-foot-deep pit. Various dark recesses within the pit lead deeper into the mountain, but whether their depth is ultimately a few feet or many miles was in no way immediately apparent. A number of boulders at

the right side of the mouth afford hand- and footholds for anyone willing to clamber down into the pit. A tree grows out of a
shelf most of the way toward the bottom, and the irregular floor
is covered with a thick accumulation of leaves.

The group we had heard before, consisting of a young man
named Chris, a young woman, a boy, and a girl, showed up
while we were assessing the scene. We chatted a little, I grabbed
some gear out of my backpack (which I took off and left behind
so as to not throw off my center of balance), and then Chris and
I descended into the pit.

The first thing we noticed was how cold it was on the floor
of the cave, just forty feet down and still exposed to the outside,
where the high that day was eighty-one degrees. Our breath
appeared before us, and I wondered just how much colder than
the prevailing fifty-five degrees (typical for caves) it was—and
why that would be the case, reflecting that an unnaturally low
prevailing temperature was a characteristic of some haunted
places. A hundred feet or so above us, a natural oculus had
opened up somewhere in the tumbled slabs of the hillside, let-
ting in more light.

Moving around on the floor of the cave's entryway and exploring the parts of it we could readily get to was somewhat hazardous and required quite a bit of attention. One misstep, while it
would almost certainly not be fatal, could very well result in a
broken ankle or some other injury that would have made getting
out of the Devil's Den difficult or impossible without considerable help.

I clambered up toward the back of the cave and one of the
main recesses that disappeared into the darkness. It was somewhat rough going, and I proceeded carefully in an attempt to
keep from hurting myself or my camera. I had, shortsightedly,
left my flashlight up above in my backpack, and, rather than
retrieve it, for the moment I decided to just slowly work my way

into the upward-twisting, narrowing passageway, periodically stopping and taking flash pictures as I went. At about the point where I could easily go no further, I took one last shot. As usual, the image I took lingered on the camera's little display for a few seconds and, as it did, something on it caught my eye but disappeared before I could focus on it. Ahead of me in the gloom, I could hear what sounded like movement of some sort, but it was probably just dripping water. Feeling an inexplicable sense of unease, I carefully extricated myself from the end of the cave and returned to the entryway.

I checked out one more of the dark recesses—a low, horizontal opening above the leafy floor and at the right side of the entryway. It led into an enclosed, rock-strewn shelf, and if there was anywhere I had seen so far in the cave where someone might have camped—both sheltered from the elements and out of sight from prying eyes above—this was it. Those features aside, it did not seem very appealing, and whether it continued further on into the hill I couldn't tell.

Needing a break, I sat down on a boulder outside the enclosed shelf and had a quick slug from my hip flask, surveying the cave as I did. There was a lot more here that warranted inspection, I reflected, and I knew I did not have the time or equipment to do it that day. I was also starting to have an eerie presentiment about something, and wanted to get out of the cave so that I could check it out.

Clambering back out of the submerged foyer to the Devil's Den onto the forested hillside, I found my way back to Diane, who was chatting with the young woman. She mentioned that she was a descendant of the Allens who were associated with this place and had returned to the area for an Allen family reunion that was taking place that weekend. In a way, her presence made the whole story about J. Sidna Allen hiding out in Devil's Den all the more immediate and tangible.

I sat down next to my wife and began to scroll through the photos I had taken, looking for one in particular. When I found it, I zoomed in as much as I could and then panned over to its left side. There, I found what I thought I had seen on the display of my camera.

At the left side of the image, at a point that would have been immediately in front of me and close enough to touch, was what appeared to be a solid, amorphous, greenish orb floating in the mouth of the passageway (I later also found a smaller, fainter orb below it in the same image, and a second image taken back into the same area from the floor of the entryway that showed at least two orbs). It struck me that something had been right next to me down in that dark pit, and that the evidence of that had been provided to me in the very seconds after I took the picture. It was, in short, the closest I have ever come to seeing in "real time" what I took to be a manifestation of lingering spiritual energy that might more commonly be referred to as a ghost.

Knowing something else was down there, something that might have been intelligent but certainly wasn't living, gave me some pause, and made me wonder if I would not perhaps be inviting trouble if I clambered straight back down into that hole and tried to see more than I already had. In a sense, I had seen more than I had a reasonable expectation to see, and our mission had thus already been a success. I decided I had done enough that day, and that further investigation would have to wait for a future expedition or another group of ghosthunters altogether.

And the question of who had died within the Devil's Den, or had enough of an emotional attachment to it that their spirit would linger within it, was a mystery into which I would have to continue to delve.

CHAPTER 20

Octagon House
MARION

An almost frightening maze of doors opened into strange-shaped rooms and halls, but the scariest doors of all, at the end of the upstairs hall, opened onto nothing. The "dark room," on the second floor, where there were dark blotches on the floor said to have been caused by the blood of slaves Abijah Thomas punished there, left an indelible impression on my boyish memory.

—Mack Sturgill, *Abijah Thomas*
and His Octagonal House

MARION IS A LONG, NARROW, antebellum town of
about 6,300 people that stretches the length of four exits along
Interstate 81 and exists largely between it and the railroad that
has served its various industries as long as anyone can remember. For those interested in Americana in general, it is named
for American Revolutionary War hero Francis "Swamp Fox"
Marion and is notable as being the birthplace of the formula for
the Mountain Dew soft drink. For ghosthunters, it is the location of a couple of sites of possible interest.

One of those—which I read about online but did not have
time to visit while en route to Abingdon and the Barter Theatre, some thirty miles further to the southwest—is the Southwestern Virginia Mental Health Institute (a.k.a., the Southwest
Lunatic Asylum). Now abandoned, it dates to the 19th century and is said to be inhabited by the spirits of patients who
died while confined there. More than one thousand of those
deceased patients are buried in unmarked graves in the cemetery located on its grounds, currently called "Forget-Me-Nots
in Heaven Cemetery," which is also reputed to be the site of
paranormal activity.

The other site is an octagonal-shaped house located a few
miles south of Marion, about halfway between the town and the
Mount Rogers National Recreation Area, at the intersection of
Thomas Bridge Road and aptly named Octagon House Road.

Better known locally as the "Round House," the "Octagon
House" was built between 1856 and 1857 by planter and entre-
preneur Abijah Thomas, who is believed to have personally
designed its custom corner bricks. He is also said to have given
the structure eight sides to make it more resistant to the wind.
Most of the other buildings in the area feature the more traditional four sides and seem resilient enough, of course, begging
the question if whether aesthetics might not have been a more
logical motivating factor.

Thomas's grandfather John—according to the book *Abijah Thomas and His Octagonal House,* written in the 1980s by local author Mack Sturgill—emigrated from Connecticut in the early 1760s and settled along the banks of the Holston River in southwestern Virginia. His son, Thomas, married and fathered ten children, the youngest of whom was Abijah. He married Priscilla Cavinette Scott in 1836, and they had a dozen children of their own and prospered in the decades leading up to the Civil War.

Abijah and Priscilla named their house "Mountain View," especially appropriate when one considers that it sits at the base of the nearby Iron Mountains and looks out at mist-shrouded Mount Rogers, the highest point in the commonwealth. It would seem that those not privileged to look out its windows are more likely to have given the place its current geometry-based labels.

Like his immediate forebears, Abijah Thomas started out as a farmer, but eventually became, in addition, a significant local manufacturer of woolen goods, leather, and iron, and controlled a great deal of property. For whatever reasons, however, he had a bad habit of not actually paying for the assets he acquired, and his debts grew—and his creditors grew more inflamed—in the years prior to, during, and after the Civil War. Fate and the legal system eventually caught up with him in a lengthy, complicated trial that began in 1869 and concluded with an 1874 decree that his assets be sold off at public auction.

When Abijah Thomas died of pneumonia at the relatively young age of 62 in 1876 he apparently still lived at the Octagon House but was penniless. Funerals had been held at the house for a number of people who had died in the years since it was built—including one for one of his daughters—and to these was added a service for its owner.

Whether these sad events contributed to the home being haunted, it is currently rumored to be, and a number of stories have been told about things people claim to have seen or otherwise experienced in the Octagon House. Many of the associated stories are based on the largely unsubstantiated premise that Thomas tortured the dozen slaves he owned, and that the property is now haunted by the tormented spirits of these unfortunates. It is just as likely, one would think, to be inhabited by the spirit of the man who fortune would have driven from it.

Visitors to the home have reported the following phenomenon: hearing strange noises throughout the building, including screams, cracking of whips, and rattling of chains; seeing blood seeping through and dripping down one of the walls; feeling a cold, tingling sensation while standing at the foot of the stairs to the second floor; and being driven out of the house or off its grounds by an angry spirit of some sort.

"This place is really haunted," one online posting from 2007 states. "I [live] right behind it, my husband and I keep up the grounds ... so we can walk our three dogs on [the] property ... [My] daughter has [photographed] an old man's face and also heard kids crying." No convenient digital images or audio recordings accompany this brief testimonial.

My wife and I visited the Octagon House on Memorial Day weekend in 2008. The crumbling, boarded-up edifice appeared in front of us suddenly as we looked for our turnoff onto the road named for it, and we turned onto the rising dirt track and began to creep along it, looking for a place to park. We passed the clearly abandoned eight-sided building and right afterward came to a small, newer, occupied house behind it (where the person who posted the message mentioned in the previous paragraph presumably lives and which, according to some sources, has been occupied since sometime during or after 2002). We used its driveway to turn around and headed back to a small, steep turnoff in front of the house that was just wide enough for one car and just long enough to get us off the road.

I collected my camera and got out of the car, while my wife proceeded to recline her seat and prop her feet up on the dashboard. I turned my attention to the two-story house and began to walk toward it through the long grass surrounding it and across patches of brick flagging that had originally been part of a circular driveway that curved up to the main entrance from either direction.

Approaching the front door, located on the west side of the building, I saw a sign indicating that the place was private property and that entry was prohibited.

Moving clockwise around the building to its next side, I came to the first of the two large ground-floor windows set into it, the first of which was uncovered and had its glass broken out, so that I could peer inside. The interior was gutted and in bad shape— the plaster completely stripped from some of the walls and from patches on the ceiling—and it had clearly been a very long time since anyone had dwelled within the place (according to one source, the building was actually condemned in the early 1970s).

I continued around the building, taking pictures as I went and looking for anything of note. As I approached the rear of the house, the three-or-so dogs in the place next door began barking, and I was glad that they did not sound very large.

At the back of the house, another one of the broken-out windows was uncovered, and when I looked through it I could see that many of the floorboards were missing and ground was showing just a few feet below their level. I reflected that some of the stories about the Octagon House had prominently featured a "haunted cellar" where slaves had been tortured and killed, but it did not appear as if one extended under the area into which I was looking, which would likely be the case if one existed at all. Likewise, there was no evidence of an exterior cellar entrance anywhere around the building, which would have been typical of a structure from this era.

Despite the lack of physical evidence for a cellar, stories persist about people who have stood at the rear of the house on the spot above where a cellar used to be and both heard screams and been confronted or driven away by an angry ghost. Whether or not these accounts are true, of course, has nothing to do with whether a cellar ever actually existed or not. And while it is certainly possible that some sort of cellar that has subsequently been filled in once existed behind the building, it is much more likely that some sort of long-gone wooden outbuilding served as the site of any atrocities that might have occurred (e.g., a summer kitchen apparently once existed directly behind the house, and a number of outbuildings, including wooden slave quarters, still stood at least into the 1930s).

Some of the accounts that cite a cellar do, in any event, seem to correspond geographically with "the large cistern to the right of the rear entrance," accordingly to the recollections of author Mack Sturgill, which "was extremely deep." This feature was not evident during my visit, but even if covered or filled in could be the focus of some psychic energy if it once was the site of some tragedy or atrocity.

A windowless "dark room" at the center of the house and on its second floor is also a prominent location for ghost stories associated with the site and has a similar reputation as a place of torment (although, according to sources cited in the Sturgill book, the room was used for storage and not punishment, the dark stains reputed to mark its floor left by the contents of broken jars of food).

I did not venture into the Octagon House, the combination of no-trespassing signs, a hazardous interior with presumably treacherous floors and stairways, and a disapproving spouse collectively serving to dissuade further investigation. I was thus unable to personally examine the "dark room" or any other parts of the house that I could not look directly into. That, along with the fact that it was a bright, sunny day in late spring, makes it not too surprising that I did not sense anything of a paranormal nature.

The Octagon House, however, does warrant further investigation by a ghosthunting group able to secure permission from the owners to explore the place (or even attempt to spend the night within it). Another story claims that visitors to the site on the night of December 1—the anniversary of Abijah Thomas's death—can witness an eerie, blue-white light moving from a nearby graveyard to the house and then back again, believed by some to be the former owner seeking in death what he lost in life. If I ever have the opportunity to expand my exploration of the site, it will probably be on that day, when any number of conditions will likely increase the chance of experiencing whatever the Octagon House has to offer.

CHAPTER 21

U.S. Route 58

LEE, SCOTT, WASHINGTON, GRAYSON, CARROLL, AND PATRICK COUNTIES

Climbing into Patrick County, Virginia's longest road becomes the "Crooked Road," a driving trail connecting the musical hot spots of Virginia's Blue Ridge Highlands. This scenic area's name comes from early explorers who found a haze over the highlands that appears blue at a distance. Here, trout streams tumble into tiny waterfalls ... as [Route] 58 curls, climbs, and becomes quite crooked, indeed.

—Joe Tennis, *Beach to Bluegrass*

WHILE IT MAY NOT BE actually haunted itself, the westernmost stretch of U.S. Route 58, which winds through some of the most rugged and beautiful terrain in the state, connects a number of strange and possibly ghost-ridden places. It is, at the very least, mysterious, special, perhaps even enchanted, and under the right conditions can seem to travelers to intersect at certain points with the unseen world.

"I don't know so much that 58 is a haunted highway," author Joe Tennis told me when we spoke about the road. And he certainly knows Route 58 as well as anyone does, having spent much of his life at various locations along its length and celebrated it in his 2007 book *Beach to Bluegrass: Places to Brake on Virginia's Longest Road*. But, he continued, "It is a very under-appreciated corridor with fascinating stories to tell." Tennis has suggested in his various works that more than one spot along its length might yet be occupied by the spirits of those who once traveled along it in life. Two such sites are in Abingdon, near the western end of Route 58.

One of these is the Barter Theatre, widely believed to be haunted by several ghosts, including that of its founder, Robert Porterfield, an actor from the Abingdon area who found himself hungry and out of work in New York City during the Great Depression. He returned home, opened the theatre, and, as its name implies, allowed local people to trade produce for theatre tickets. His spirit has been seen in the theatre many times (Barter Theatre is the subject of its own chapter in this book).

Another is the Martha Washington Inn, a historic hotel established in what was once a women's college that has been the site of many ghostly phenomena. The spirit most often said to haunt the inn, often referred to as "Beth," is believed to have been a student nurse at what was then known as Martha Washington College when the Civil War began and it was converted to a hospital. When one of the wounded men she cared for was dying, he asked her to play her violin for him, and she complied. To this day, many people have said, her music can still be heard, especially in room 403 and on nights when the moon is full. Some people have even claimed to have seen her. A number of other ghosts, including one of a maimed and bleeding Civil War soldier, have also been spotted at the inn.

My wife and I spent part of Memorial Day weekend 2008 in Abingdon, and spent some time at the Barter Theatre when we were there. Our investigation there concluded, we headed out along Route 58 on an eastward journey that would ultimately take us to the Devil's Den Nature Preserve and the haunted courthouse at Hillsville (both of which are covered in separate chapters of this book).

Route 58 is an east-west U.S. highway that runs through Virginia for some five-hundred miles, from the far southwestern corner of the state that meets both Kentucky and Tennessee, all the way across the southern edge of the Old Dominion to Virginia Beach. It is, in fact, the longest road in the state. Historic communities through which it passes on its journey through the mountains, the Piedmont, and ultimately down to the sea include Bristol, Abingdon, Galax, Danville, Emporia, Franklin, Suffolk, Chesapeake, Portsmouth, Norfolk, and Virginia Beach, all of which, of course, have their own ghost stories (e.g., the ones associated with Berry Hill Road and the Wreck of the Old 97 in Danville, both the subjects of chapters in this book).

Much of what was opened in 1931 as U.S. Route 58 was originally called State Route 12 and was part of the 1918 state highway system, which generally followed the current highway eastward from Abingdon to Virginia Beach. The stretch that is now part of Route 58 west of Abingdon was in those old days part of State Route 10.

An eastern, two-lane section of the highway between Emporia and Suffolk was at one time known as "The Suicide Strip," as a result of the high number of fatal accidents that occurred along it (which decreased significantly when traffic was separated by the addition of a second roadway in the early 1990s). No such nickname seems to have been applied to the mountainous and even more treacherous western sections, which would seem more than anything else to be more a function of the road passing there through a much less densely populated area. Tragedies of the sort associated with highway accidents have, in any event, certainly produced any number of local ghost stories along the length of the road overall.

My first experience with Route 58 was in October 2002, when I was driving west along it toward Bristol in search of a place to spend the night, having climbed nearby Mount Rogers earlier that day. A storm of unprecedented fury struck that night, and lashed the forests around me as I crawled up and down along the winding road in the darkness. Great bands of lightning erupted over the ridgelines, illuminating in fairy fire the tortured landscape and leaping from hill to hill like the very devils of Appalachian folklore. (My wife, Diane, actually crossed my path in a manner of speaking that night, having likely flown right overhead on her way back to Washington, D.C., from a business trip. She can still recall looking down and seeing the strange, powerful, lightning formations erupting over the darkened landscape below her, and it was heartening to know she had been nearby during my journey.)

That was a pretty exhilarating experience, and I was glad for the opportunity to drive along that stretch of road again. Unlike my first experience, we were blessed with the characteristically beautiful weather that we experienced while doing most of the fieldwork for this book as we picked up Route 58 from where it intersects with I-81 and began following it southeastward. The road is known there locally as J.E.B. Stuart Highway, and, as we were to discover, it would have many other names just along the length we drove that day—sometimes as many as four at once. That is a peculiarity of the Old Dominion, where it seems just about any local jurisdiction can name a road whatever it wants. At one point, for example, in addition to being called Route 58 and J.E.B. Stuart Highway, the road was also labeled Wilson Highway, A.L. Philpott Memorial Highway, and possibly any number of other things as well.

Just a couple of miles into our journey, we passed a road leading down to a streambed, and I noticed it was called Drowning Ford Road. Unless it was named after a local family named "Drowning," I reflected, it probably had some ghost stories of its own. And someone who could spend enough time along an old highway like this and wanted to hear the stories could probably find hundreds of them eventually.

After about ten miles we passed through Damascus, a little mountain town at the edge of where Route 58 enters the Mount Rogers National Recreation Area, and I decided to stop and top off our tank and pick up a few provisions, not knowing how many amenities would be available on the road ahead of us. Damascus is an old town, founded in the 18th century after Daniel Boone blazed a trail through where it sits. Among the many old and strange stories associated with it are tales of Mary, a 19th-century witch whose spirit some believe still haunts the wooded hills around the town.

Once we left Damascus, the relatively straight road we had been driving on disappeared. Thereafter, Route 58 proceeded in three dimensions, moving up wooded slopes and down into sunlit gullies, heading generally east but cutting sharply north or south or even back in the direction from which it had come for short stretches. Frequently, the wooded terrain to our left—along the eastern approaches to the Iron Mountains and in the direction of Mount Rogers—sloped upward sharply, while the ground to our right fell off equally precipitously into little valleys cut through with sparkling streams. Sometimes, wooded heights surrounded us on all sides, towering over the road like some great sylvan arcade. We were struck with a profound impression of wildness and beauty that affected us very favorably and was as different from my previous experience with the road as it could have been.

Signs to be heeded along this segment of Route 58 are speed markers, which frequently called for speeds of 25 miles per hour and, in some cases, speeds as low as 15 miles per hour. Exceeding those speeds in anything less than ideal conditions could very likely reveal the treacherousness of the rugged, wooded terrain in a tragic way.

Signs less believable were those indicating distances to various towns ahead of us, including Galax, which successively went from 57, to 59, to 56. Presumably, these numbers were supposed to indicate the number of miles along the road to the points in question, and should thus not have gotten larger the further one went along the road, vicissitudes of terrain notwithstanding. During a nighttime trip by oneself, quirks like this would definitely have seemed disquietingly eerie and made one wonder if they had not somehow got turned around in the darkness.

During our journey along Route 58, we periodically passed occupied homes and farms, as well as the entrances to several state, county, and regional parks. That the area had a low population density was attested to by the Mount Rogers Unified School, a building constructed of mountain stone that has served kindergarten through twelfth grade since the 1930s. That the road was once much more significant as a commercial arterial that has been supplanted by the interstates was attested to by the many abandoned service stations we passed—perhaps as many as fifteen in a sixty-mile stretch. We passed through any number of tiny ghost hamlets as well, little clusters of boarded up buildings at lonely road junctions that had not seen life for many years.

Route 58 has its share of abandoned buildings.

Shortly after passing through Independence, we turned off north onto Riverside Drive, a loop of maybe fifteen miles that traces the beautiful New River and reconnects with Route 58 a few miles further east. We were following up on rumors we had heard of an ostensibly haunted bridge dubbed "Lovers' Leap" by some, where two young, star-crossed lovers, their families at odds with each other, decided to become unified in death rather than remain separated in life. According to the legends, anyone passing over the span might spot the spectral images a young woman, a young man, or both together, variously calling out to each other or jumping individually or in tandem off of the bridge. We did not see any of that, but did remark upon what a melancholy spot it was, the rusting metal girders suspended over the placid river, collapsing ruins in the wood line near its north end, an ad hoc memorial to the victims of a more recent traffic accident set up at its south. A more formal and presumably nighttime investigation might very well turn up more. ("Lovers' leaps" are, by the way, something of a state institution.

As author Joe Tennis has observed: "All over the Old Dominion, so many cliffs are called Lovers' Leap that the state's motto should be 'Virginia is for Leaping Lovers,' rather than the more familiar 'Virginia is for Lovers.'")

Early in the afternoon we reached Galax, the first relatively large town we had seen since leaving Abingdon, and sought out Harmon's Outlet, a local Western store located right on Route 58 (which was known there as Carrollton Pike). Deena McKinney, proprietor of the Volunteer Gap Inn, where we would be staying that night, had directed us to the outfitter and told us that it had one of the area's better museums of local history right in its back room! We confirmed that she was right, and, after wending our way through a shelf maze of jeans and boots, spent some time browsing the long, musty room of exhibits and historic newspaper clippings. I was especially interested in the wealth of material devoted to the 1912 shooting at the Carroll County Courthouse in Hillsville, a reputedly haunted location that we would be visiting the next day. No one at the store could or would tell us anything about local ghost stories, however (a phenomena we were to experience consistently in this area).

Not long after leaving Galax we reached the juncture of Route 58 and I-77. After a brief stop for lunch, we left the historic and storied older highway and turned south onto the newer, more efficient, and considerably more austere modern road, which would take us just a short distance south to our next stop, the Devil's Den Nature Preserve (a subject of a chapter unto itself in this book).

There are a number of other promising locations along the Route 58 corridor of potential interest to ghosthunters that we were not able to visit on this particular expedition, but which we hoped to see on future trips.

One of these is Laurel Hill, the boyhood home of Confederate Major General J.E.B. Stuart, Robert E. Lee's flamboyant cavalry commander, located south of Route 58 and about ten miles outside the town of Claudville. "I would give anything to make a pilgrimage to the old place, and when the war is over quietly spend the rest of my days there," Stuart told his brother in 1863. Sadly, he fell in combat in May 1864 at the Battle of Yellow Tavern near Richmond, a year before the war ended, and was never able to enjoy the rest he yearned for. Since then, stories have been told about sightings of his ghost at the estate, seeking in death the comfort he was deprived of in life.

Another site that might warrant some attention is Fairy Stone State Park, a few miles north of Route 58 near Stuart. It is famous as a source of a rare sort of mineral structure popularly dubbed "fairy stones," which variously take the form of St. Andrew's, Roman, and Maltese crosses. According to psychic researcher Ian Alan, these stones can bestow upon the person carrying them a multitude of benefits, depending on their form, which include "great physical and mental prowess," "the ability to traverse ... heaven and hell," and "the power of precognitive sight, hearing, and the gift of invisibility" (he has also suggested that once benefiting from a stone but then setting it aside can draw the unwelcome attentions of ghosts and consequent negative effects). Teddy Roosevelt and Thomas Edison both subscribed to these beliefs at least in part and carried stones accordingly. Assuming some truth behind these stories, a site that could produce such spiritually potent objects would seem to be worthy of attention by investigators of the paranormal.

While we did not see everything we wanted to, there was also no question that our journey along Route 58 had been markedly more enjoyable than the trip along I-81 we had taken into southwestern Virginia during the first two days of our trip that weekend, and confirmed my belief that—time permitting—local highways were always preferable to interstates in any number of ways.

Whether Route 58 is or is not actually a haunted highway per se, it does link numerous spots that likely are the haunts of ghosts, and I would be surprised if some investigation did not turn up paranormal phenomena along certain spots of the roadway itself. And, beyond being a useful thoroughfare for those interested in hunting ghosts in some of the most isolated parts of the Old Dominion, it is a beautiful and picturesque means of reaching them.

VALLEY

VIRGINIA: VALLEY

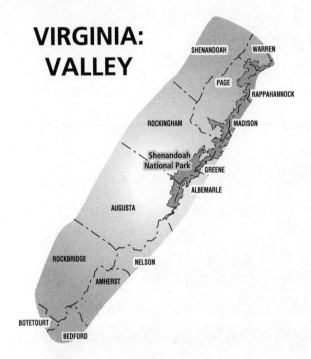

Frederick, Shenandoah, and Warren Counties
   Cedar Creek Battlefield

Lexington
   Virginia Military Institute

Middletown
   Belle Grove Plantation
   The Wayside Inn

Rockbridge County
   Poor House Tunnel Road

Winchester
   Virginia's Most Haunted City

CHAPTER 22

Belle Grove Plantation
MIDDLETOWN

"As soon as I started down the driveway leading to the mansion, I sensed a ghost. I also sensed a terrible fight between two women on a dark rainy day, and a gruesome murder. I felt all this before I started the tour. And when the tour was over, I had the very strong sensation that a woman ghost followed us down and out of the house."

—L. B. Taylor Jr., "The Vengeful Return
of Hetty Cooley"

ONE WINTRY EVENING in late 1860 or early 1861, the mistress of Belle Grove was found severely beaten in the plantation's smokehouse. She was only semiconscious, groaning helplessly in pain, unable to pull her feet out of the building's smoldering fire pit. Much of her hair had been burned off and her head and face were bleeding from multiple wounds and had been beaten and singed almost beyond recognition. Her nose and right cheekbone were shattered, one eye was sunken into her head, and the other protruded unnaturally. She had also been choked, as evidenced by the finger marks on her throat. Four days later, she succumbed to her wounds and died without identifying her attacker.

Hetty Cooley had lived at Belle Grove for just a short time when she was attacked, and the story of the events that had apparently led to her violent death had unfolded only a matter of months earlier.

Sometime in 1860, on the eve of the Civil War that would ravage the surrounding valley, bachelor Benjamin Cooley had taken possession of Belle Grove, a grain and livestock farm, and moved into it with a small staff of servants and slaves. Within a few months, he met and then married Hetty, an attractive widow, and brought her to live with him at his new home.

Hetty began to have problems almost immediately with one of her husband's house slaves, a young woman named Harriette Robinson who served as cook and housekeeper and was impertinent, physically intimidating, and feared by her fellow servants. According to the eventual testimony of other household staff, Harriette hated Hetty from the start, was openly disobedient to her, and made threats against her to others, expressing among other things a desire to poison her.

Tension mounted between the two women and reached a crescendo when the slave vehemently accused her mistress of stealing from her and of lying when she denied this. This apparently drove Hetty beyond the point of what she could tolerate, and she grabbed a broomstick and began to beat Harriette, who fought back. The two were grappling on the floor when other members of the household rushed in and pulled them away from each other.

Things having reached an intolerable point, Hetty implored her husband to get rid of the hostile and disobedient Harriette. For reasons unknown, however, Benjamin declined to do so.

A pall descended over Belle Grove after this, and a fearful Hetty confided to a friend named Mary Moore, who was staying at the estate, that she did not believe she would live much longer.

One afternoon soon thereafter, Hetty and Mary were sitting in the parlor of Belle Grove when the mistress of the house excused herself and went outside to attend to something. When she had not returned more than two hours later, Mary became concerned and began to look for her. When she could not find her, she asked one of the estate's tenant farmers, James Gordon, and some of the resident slaves to help her look (Benjamin apparently being away from Belle Grove on some business).

One of the searchers heard groaning coming from inside the smokehouse but, when he tried to investigate, discovered that the door was locked. A desperate hunt for the key ensued, and, when it was found, the search party opened the door. They were greeted by the stench of burning hair and the sight of the savagely maimed and beaten Hetty.

Harriette was, naturally, the prime suspect in the attack and was arrested and tried. A preponderance of evidence and testimony from people who had heard the young woman's threats against her mistress led to a quick conviction. Her precise sentence is today unclear, but records indicate she died sometime thereafter while in prison.

Belle Grove has long had a reputation for being haunted, and if anything could account for this, a sordid, violent episode like the murder of Hetty Cooley—leading to two untimely deaths—certainly could. The history of the plantation, however, predates the killing by more than six decades, and it is certainly possible that previous generations of owners also made their own contributions to whatever spiritual energy may continue to linger in it.

In 1794, Major Isaac Hite, Jr., an alumnus of William and Mary College and a veteran of the Continental Army during the Revolutionary War, began construction on Belle Grove, using limestone quarried on the surrounding property. He was the grandson of one of the original German immigrants who had settled in the northern Shenandoah Valley, and he built upon a 483-acre tract of land that his father had given him in 1783 as a wedding gift when he married Nelly Madison, sister of future President James Madison. The stately home—which incorporates elements of Classical Revival and the architectural canons of Thomas Jefferson and features interior woodwork in a transitional style ranging from Georgian to Federal—was completed in 1797. It was, in short, as stylish and up-to-date as any fine home in the valley.

Nelly died just five years after the house was completed, having borne three children, and Hite was remarried to Ann Maury, with whom he had another ten children. Needing room to accommodate this growing brood, Hite added an extension at the west end of the house in 1815, increasing its length to a full one hundred feet.

Hite also continued to expand the plantation itself, eventually increasing his holdings to 7,500 acres, a general store, a gristmill, a sawmill, a distillery, and a workforce of more than one hundred slaves.

By the time Hite died in 1836, his empire had already started to recede a bit and, after Ann followed him fifteen years later, Belle Grove and its property were sold off to various owners outside of their family, their significant progeny notwithstanding. Benjamin Cooley acquired the house in 1860 and, in the war years that followed, it served variously as the headquarters of Confederate General Stonewall Jackson and Union General Philip Sheridan and was at the middle of the savage Battle of Cedar Creek. A number of other owners followed over the ensuing decades.

Today, Belle Grove appears much as it did in the late-18th and

**Belle Grove today appears much as it did
in the late-18th and early-19th centuries.**

early-19th centuries and is a National Historic Landmark, a Virginia
Historic Landmark, and a historic property of the National Trust for
Historic Preservation. Its features include the mansion itself, original outbuildings, a 1918 barn, an overseer's house, and a slave cemetery, as well as gardens, fields, meadows, and an apple orchard.

My wife and I visited Belle Grove Plantation in April 2008 during a ghosthunting expedition to the northern Shenandoah Valley.
The various charms of the place were not enough to induce her to get
out of the car, and, as I walked through the parking area, out of the
corner of my eye I could see a small pair of feet appear on the pas-
senger side of the windshield. Assuming these were not the spectral
extremities of Hetty Cooley, I continued on toward the house.

Several female docents ranging from teenaged to grandmo-
therly were present in the entry area and gift shop when I went into
the main building, and I approached one of them and told her what

my interests were. She responded by informing me that the director of the museum discourages the staff from telling ghost stories
or expressing a belief that Belle Grove is haunted. She believed it
was, however, based on her experiences and those of others who
work at the plantation, and agreed to talk with me on condition of
anonymity.

"There was an attack on the property," she said, confirming
the published account of the incident that I had read, "and one
of the slaves actually attacked the wife of the home's owner." She
was a little fuzzy as to whether the brutally beaten woman had
been found in the smokehouse or the icehouse, but details like that
don't actually have much to do with the essential truth or falsity
of a tale. She went on to confirm the story of the conflict between
the mistress of Belle Grove and the impertinent slave who was
convicted of mortally beating her.

"Her ghost actually wanders around here," she said of the murdered woman. When I asked for an example of this spirit's manifestation, she told me a story she was personally familiar with.

They had the carpets and rugs taken up and cleaned a couple
of years ago. Once they had been cleaned and were ready to be
returned, Belle Grove staff arranged to have them delivered on a
Saturday before 5 P.M., which is when the site normally closes.

"The driver was running late, and got here about six, after
everyone was gone," my source explained. Hoping to find someone to whom he could turn over his truckload of floor coverings,
he came up and knocked on the front door. A lady in period dress
opened up the door, and didn't say anything to him, even when
he identified himself and asked where she wanted him to drop off
the carpets, merely pointing silently to a spot down the hall. So, he
carried the carpets in and put them down where the lady had indicated. The docent continued, "She didn't say anything to him the
whole time, and he said he felt that was kind of odd," but accepted
that, for whatever reason, she might just not have wanted to say

anything. He thanked her for her help and then left.

"The next day, when the docent in charge came in and opened up," she discovered that all the carpets had been delivered, my source said. "She called the cleaning company and asked them when they had delivered them. They put the driver on the phone with her," and he explained what had happened.

The docent in charge was, understandably, shaken, and verified that the alarms had not been tampered with and that none of the staff had been at the house the previous evening after it had closed. She, and many of her coworkers—among them the docent I spoke with—believe that the driver had encountered the unquiet spirit of Hetty Cooley. Similar incidents have convinced them that Belle Grove is indeed haunted and that the ghosts of its previous inhabitants continue to walk its halls. Yet other stories involve Civil War soldiers and are similar to those told about the Cedar Creek Battlefield in general.

While I did not experience anything out of the ordinary at Belle Grove, I do believe that other people have and that it is a site of probable significance to anyone interested in haunted sites. Visitors with such interests, however, will need to be a bit circumspect in their inquiries if they want to obtain any useful information. And, unless something changes in the attitudes of the people in charge of the site, no one is likely to get permission to do a formal investigation or anything out of the ordinary (e.g., an overnight stay). Even my cordial letter to the president of Belle Grove Plantation's board of trustees, requesting some statement on whether or not the place is likely haunted, was simply ignored.

It is a little off-putting that the people running the place are so set on discouraging an interest in any ghosts that might inhabit the property and—like too many people in positions of authority in a country where freedom of expression is supposed to be sacrosanct—try to control what others think and say. Indeed, this desire to hide the story of Hetty Cooley is strong enough to induce the current masters of Belle Grove to forego mentioning not just the story but the fact that the Cooley family ever dwelled at the estate in the information they make available about it (facts that can, nonetheless, be discovered and confirmed independently). However, ghosts may be less inclined to stay silent when they have something to say. And, by all accounts, the ghosts of Belle Grove have spoken, and doubtless will continue to speak, to those who want to hear to them.

CHAPTER 23

Cedar Creek Battlefield
FREDERICK, SHENANDOAH, AND WARREN COUNTIES

Up from the South at break of day,
Bringing to Winchester fresh dismay,
The affrighted air with a shudder bore,
Like a herald in haste, to the chieftain's door,
The terrible grumble, and rumble, and roar,
Telling the battle was on once more,
And Sheridan twenty miles away.

— Thomas Buchanan Read, "Sheridan's Ride"

IN THE FOGGY, PREDAWN DARKNESS of October 19, 1864, the Confederate Army of the Valley under Leiutenant

184

General Jubal A. Early had surprised the numerically superior Union army at Cedar Creek and quickly routed the troops of its VIII and XIX Army Corps. Alerted to the debacle while about twenty miles away in Winchester, Major General Philip Sheridan, the Federal commander, raced to the battlefield to rally his troops (as commemorated in the wartime poem "Sheridan's Ride").

"Little Phil" succeeded in halting the rout of his troops, rallied them, and, that afternoon, led a crushing counterattack against the rebel forces, driving them from the battlefield and regaining control of it for the Northern army. Overall, the fierce, back-and-forth conflict spilled into three counties (Frederick, Shenandoah, and Warren), involved some 52,945 men (31,945 U.S. and 21,000 C.S.), and inflicted an estimated 8,575 casualties (5,665 U.S. and 2,910 C.S.).

Sheridan's success at Cedar Creek produced an unqualified Union victory and broke the back of the Confederate army in the region and was the high-water mark of his Shenandoah Valley Campaign, which continued until December 1864. That campaign, along with Sherman's successes in Georgia, gave Lincoln the momentum he needed to win reelection to a second term in the White House.

Cedar Creek Battlefield is, by all accounts, a virtual hotbed of spiritual activity and should rank high on the lists of stops for ghosthunters traveling through the Old Dominion. When my wife and I visited Cedar Creek, we went straight to the Cedar Creek Battlefield Foundation's visitor center, located on the Valley Pike—the road down which Sheridan had rushed from Winchester to reinforce the crumbling Union line—a few miles outside of Middletown.

"I'm just going to wait in the car," she said, reclining her seat as I opened my door to get out.

"I know, Hon," I responded, as usual. "I won't be long."

And I wasn't.

The two men staffing the visitor's center were certainly friendly enough and were forthcoming with information of the sort likely to be of use to a conventional visitor. When I explained that my visit was for purposes of researching a book on ghost-hunting in Virginia and that I planned to devote an entire chapter of it to the Cedar Creek Battlefield, however, their demeanors cooled. They gave me the business card of the foundation's current executive director and told me that any questions I had along my lines of interest needed to be addressed exclusively to her. (After I got home I wrote a detailed and cordial letter to the executive director of the foundation in hopes of obtaining an official statement about the many ghost stories associated with the battlefield, but I received no reply.)

Despite the reticence of the Cedar Creek Battlefield Foundation, innumerable ghostly sightings and stories of hauntings have been associated with the battlefield over the years, making it a key site for inclusion in this book. Such stories have been written about by ghost researcher L.B. Taylor Jr., who in the 1980s and 1990s wrote dozens of books about haunted sites in Virginia. A number of specific sites on or near the battlefield, including Belle Grove Plantation and the Wayside Inn, both covered in this book, also have rich bodies of ghostly lore associated with them, in part as a result of the battle.

Such stories began in the years immediately following the war, and included accounts by local farmers of spectral soldiers battling hand to hand in the streambeds of Cedar Creek and fields surrounding it.

Stories also began to be told of strange sightings at the Episcopal church now known as St. Thomas Chapel in Middletown, where coffins of slain soldiers had remained stacked for more than a month after the battle. These started when morbid curiosity seekers opened some of the coffins and, according to their accounts, discovered bodies that had not begun to decompose even after four or five weeks. Such stories grew to include widespread reports of ghostly candle lights moving around in the church even when it was devoid of people; phantasmal groaning and footsteps; military band music emanating from the empty house of worship; and strange, unidentifiable animals the size of calves lurking about the site.

Other phenomena have included sightings of soldiers, individually or in squads, marching across the battlefield in the gloom of twilight; sounds of cavalry units trotting along its country roads in the darkness; and various tales of barn-haunting specters and headless troopers (a la Washington Irving).

Sightings of these sorts seem to have reached a peak about a century ago (at least as far as the written record is concerned). One published, if somewhat whimsical, theory is that the ongoing tilling, planting, and harvesting of the fields has gradually driven the ghosts away (an explanation that, even if it is not true, has a certain poetical elegance). Many acres of the battlefield remain untilled, however, and tales of hauntings and ghostly sightings persist into our era and seem to be on the rise again.

As bloody as Cedar Creek was, other battles have been as bad or worse, and it is anyone's guess why there have been so many reports of ghostly sightings at Cedar Creek in the more than 140 years since the battle was fought there.

Ghost spoor, however, is not generally evident on bright, sunny days, and we did not notice anything otherworldly during our brief visit to the Cedar Creek Battlefield. Night, fog, solitude, and any number of other ghost-friendly factors would, presumably, have made us more receptive to the presence of lurking spirits during our visit to the site.

CHAPTER 24

Poor House Road Tunnel
ROCKBRIDGE COUNTY

We recorded a really strange EVP of what sounds to me like a young child very close to the microphone. ... I have been working with EVP for about three years and have never had one quite like this before, [which] seems to be of a young child saying "reach you ..." This was recorded and analyzed before knowing the background and, to be honest, I was actually quite shocked to learn of the tragedy involving the young children.

—Terri Vanderlaan, Virginia Paranormal

SOME OF THE CREEPIEST and most probably haunted places are not those that are regularly seen by the living, but rather those lonely spots that people rarely pass through. One of these is certainly the tunnel on Poor House Road, a passageway of cut-stone blocks through an overgrown and unused railway embankment located on a forlorn stretch of wooded road north of Lexington.

While it is not very far off the beaten path, Poor House Road is sufficiently removed from main thoroughfares to keep most people from being aware of it, and to ensure that many people in the local area familiar with its reputation are not even sure exactly where it is. It intersects with a winding and little-used stretch of the old Valley Pike that splits off for a short distance from Route 11, along which most noninterstate traffic moves north and south through the valley.

My wife and I had learned about the Poor House Road tunnel in a detailed account posted online by Terri Vanderlaan of Virginia Paranormal, a ghosthunting group that had visited it in December 2007. We had read in that report, and from people we spoke with in Lexington, a wide range of urban legends associated with the place. These included it being a site for lynchings in years past; a story about two little girls who had been playing nearby in the woods when an unknown person shot them to death; and an account of a woman who had been raped and killed in the tunnel. Like most urban legends, whether true or not, the veracity of these stories is almost impossible to verify. We also uncovered a number of accounts about apparent paranormal phenomena, which included sightings of the spectral figure of a man who was killed by a train on the tracks above; a mist that is supposed to rise up around anyone standing in the middle of the tunnel; and the illusion of car headlights coming up behind people sitting in the tunnel at midnight, who then experience engine failure when they try to start their cars and get out of the way.

With such a rich body of associated lore, whether it was true or not, we decided the site warranted some investigation while we were in the Lexington area visiting Virginia Military Institute.

So, around 5 P.M. on May 23, 2008, we left the VMI campus and headed north up Route 11, out of town, and soon thereafter onto the short Valley Pike bypass. Near its north end, we came to the intersection with Poor House Road.

Poor House Road is a short, semi-improved, gravel-topped track flanked by heavy vegetation that has one end at its intersection with the Valley Pike and winds to its end at Reid Road, just a mile and a quarter to the northwest. It is barely more than a single lane wide, which, along with being rough, meant we found it advisable to watch our speed and keep as far to the right as possible (and that we were glad to be in an SUV). We passed one house but did not meet any oncoming traffic, however, by the time the tunnel loomed up on the road in front of us.

I parked a few hundred feet short of the tunnel. I got out of the car, grabbed my camera, and looped its strap over my neck. Diane indicated she was "just going to wait in the car," and I heard its doors lock behind me as I walked away from it.

It was very quiet as I walked toward the south end of the tunnel, and I could not hear anything but the crunch of my hiking sneakers on the cinder road and the gurgling of a small stream that appeared to flow through the tunnel along its west side from the north. No other sounds came to me from the surrounding woods, which had spread over the years onto the crest of the embankment and choked the tracks along which trains had once run.

As I started to enter the tunnel, I stopped suddenly and an involuntary chill of fright ran up my spine as I suddenly heard voices ahead of me! I could see through to the other end of the short passageway, however, and could not make out anybody in the gloom. I strained to listen to what sounded like two or more men engaged in discussion, but could not make out any individual words, the exchange being muffled like a conversation heard through the wall of an adjoining room. I crept forward slowly, straining to listen, and as I did the words dissolved into the echoing trickle of the water flowing through the tunnel and were gone.

I moved slowly into the tunnel, the cobbled surface of which was heavily rutted and pooled with water. As I proceeded to take some pictures about midway through the tunnel, I wished I had thought to bring a flashlight with me, not so much to help me navigate my way through the damp culvert as to make out the spray-painted graffiti on the walls and more accurately line up some shots of it. I paused in the middle and waited to see if a mist would start to rise up around me, more than half expecting that it would. There was a strange haziness around the edges of the tunnel entrances, but it seemed more likely to be a trick of the light than anything else. I continued through to the far end of the tunnel.

Back outside, I walked a few hundred feet up the road, took some pictures of the tunnel from its north end, and then walked back toward it.

As I came within about twenty feet of the tunnel, I was once again stunned to hear voices coming from it. This time, I had the impression that I was hearing two or more women speaking in frantic voices but, as before, I could not make out individual words. The sounds faded as I tried to make them out and headed back into the tunnel, once again dissolving into the sound of the trickling water. I continued through the tunnel again, taking pictures as I went and starting once when I thought I felt something brush against me in the darkness (which was probably nothing more than me coming into contact with the nearby wall).

I walked quickly back to the car and told Diane what I had experienced. None of it tempted her to get out of the car and accompany me on foot into the tunnel, but she did not object when I said we should drive through to the other side. We stopped about halfway through and I rolled down the windows to see if we could hear anything unusual, but the only sounds that came to us were those of the engine and trickling water.

We parked a few hundred feet up the road on the north side of the tunnel. I stuffed my microcassette recorder into my pocket, and I headed back toward the dark passageway, turning on the recorder as I approached it.

The third time I entered the tunnel on foot, I heard a cacophony of voices—like they were coming from a crowd of people that, by this time, I knew were in no physical sense in the darkness before me—and also had a sensation of music. When I strained to listen carefully and isolate something distinct, the sounds once again melted away into the gurgling of the water flowing around me.

I walked about two-thirds of the way through the tunnel, taking pictures as I went, and then thought I heard something in the direction of the car, so I trotted back toward it. All it had been was the engine of our hybrid SUV kicking on, but both of us were pretty much ready to go, so I got back in the car and we drove up the narrow, vegetation-choked road to find a place where we could turn around. We then drove back toward the tunnel, went back through it, and headed back toward Lexington to find a place to spend the night.

The December 2007 ghosthunting group had obtained several bits of electronic evidence of a spiritual presence at the Poor House Road tunnel, including photos that showed bright streaks of light inside the tunnel and ghost orbs outside of it, and audio recordings of voice-like sounds. My own photographs did not reveal anything similar, and neither Diane nor I would make out anything distinct in my audio recordings (although some of the sounds were evocative to me of the things I thought I had heard when in the tunnel).

Two of the digital photos I had taken from the middle of the tunnel toward its north end during my last walk into it, however, were somewhat peculiar. In one, the sunlit vegetation framed in the mouth of the tunnel was flattened out and a little streaky, like an Impressionist painting (and similar to the some of the effects that can be applied to an image on a computer with a graphics program). In the other, the appearance of the woods outside the tunnel was similar to that in the first, but the mouth of the tunnel was bent downward along its right edge and upward along its bottom edge—as if its bottom right corner were being pinched—and a wedge-shaped segment of floor had taken on the appearance of dark waves, making it look as if it might have been taken from inside a sea cave.

I certainly don't expect that a couple of odd photos and an impression of indistinct voices should convince anyone else that any particular place is a haunt of troubled spirits. But of all the places I visited while researching this book, the tunnel on Poor House Road is the one that gave me the greatest sense of disquiet when I was there. And it is one of few that still raises the hair on the back of my neck and sends shivers up my spine when I recall the voices I heard and examine the strange photos that I carried out of it.

In this image, the sunlit vegetation framed in the mouth of the tunnel was flattened out and a little streaky, like an Impressionist painting.

CHAPTER 25

Virginia Military Institute
LEXINGTON

All [VMI] cadets ... are required to live in the Barracks. Running under these castlelike structures is an underground netherworld known as "the Catacombs." The strange, mysterious noises coming from the dark, dank cellars have never been satisfactorily explained. Neither has the frightening presence that has terrified many courageous cadets ... [an] otherworldly thing [that] is said to have a hideous yellow face with a scar that bleeds.

—Daniel W. Barefoot, *Haunted Halls of Ivy*

OFTEN REFERRED TO AS THE "West Point of the South," Virginia Military Institute has a rich history that began decades before to the Civil War and is inextricably linked to the history of the state whose name it bears. A highly ranked academic institution that combines an austere, physically demanding environment with strict discipline, it is the oldest state-supported military college in the United States. It is also likely among the most haunted colleges in the country.

VMI was founded on November 11, 1839, on the site of the Virginia state arsenal in the city of Lexington. Its first graduating class, that of 1842, was relatively small, and included just sixteen cadets. The school grew steadily, and in 1850 construction began on new barracks, allowing the corps of cadets to expand. A year later, Thomas "Stonewall" Jackson—the man who was to become its most revered faculty member—came to the college as professor of Natural and Experimental Philosophy.

Jackson had not yet acquired his *nom de guerre* at that point, of course, and was only a major when in 1859 he led cadets into what is now West Virginia to help suppress abolitionist John Brown's rebellion (they arrived in Charles Town in good time to see the fiery insurrectionist hanged).

In the years that followed, VMI cadets and alumni played a critical role both in training Confederate military forces and directly participating in combat. Cadets were called to active military service fourteen different times during the Civil War and, under the leadership of Jackson, were sent to train recruits at Camp Lee in Richmond. Fifteen alumni rose to the rank of general in the Southern armies, and VMI graduates were considered to be some of the best officers in both the Confederate and Union forces (many of them remaining loyal to the U.S. government even after secession).

VMI's proudest moment occurred on May 15, 1864, at the Battle of New Market, when cadets, ranging in age from fourteen to twenty-two, fought as an independent unit, a first in U.S.

military history. General John C. Breckinridge, commander of
the Confederate forces, held the young men in reserve as long
as he could, committing them to battle only after Federal troops
broke through his lines.

"Put the boys in," Breckinridge commanded as he saw
the Union forces taking control of the battlefield, "and may
God forgive me for the order." Not only did the cadets hold the
line, however, they eventually managed to advance, capturing
a Union artillery emplacement and winning the battle for the
Confederacy. In the process, they suffered ten killed in action
and forty-two wounded.

The following month, during the Valley Campaigns of
1864, Union forces shelled and burned VMI, almost completely
destroying the campus and forcing it to temporarily move its
classes to Richmond (cannonballs can still be seen embedded
in the stone walls of some of the buildings). When the capitol
of the Confederacy was evacuated in April 1865, the corps of
cadets was disbanded until after the end of the war.

Today, the VMI campus covers 134 acres—12 of them designated as the Virginia Military Institute Historic District and
listed on the National Register of Historic Places—and is home
to more than 1,300 cadets during the school year.

All cadets are housed in the sprawling, five-story New Barracks, which was completed in 1949 (the Old Barracks, now designated a National Historic Landmark, stands on the site of the
arsenal upon which VMI was founded). Its two wings surround
a pair of quadrangles connected by a sally port, and all of the
rooms open onto stoops facing one of these quadrangles. Four
arched entryways lead into the barracks, and these are named
for George Washington, Stonewall Jackson, George Marshall,
and Jonathan Daniels (a VMI graduate and Episcopal seminar-
ian who was killed in 1965 as a result of his participation in the
Civil Rights movement).

With such a colorful history, it is little wonder that so many

The statue known as "Virginia Mourning Her Dead"

ghost stories, paranormal phenomena, and local superstitions have become associated with VMI in the years since the Civil War.

One of the most well known involves the statue "Virginia Mourning Her Dead," by sculptor Moses Ezekiel—himself a VMI graduate who was among those injured at the Battle of New Market—beside which are buried six of the cadets slain in the battle, the other four resting at places of their families' choosing (although all ten are honored with markers). The statue is located near the center of campus, where people have reported hearing groans issue forth from the life-sized statue of a grieving woman and to have seen tears flowing from her metallic eyes.

Another of the most famous phenomena associated with the institution—although, while paranormal, it is by no means clear if it is ghostly in nature—is the massive painting in Jackson Memorial Hall by Benjamin West Clinedinst depicting the charge of the VMI cadets at the Battle of New Market. Many people who have found themselves alone in the three-story Gothic Revival chapel have claimed to see the figures begin to move across the surface of the picture, and to hear the sounds of battle emanate from it.

Other legends related to the painting state that anyone in the building alone at midnight who touches the painting and then turns around will see spectral figures in the seats behind them (either the cadets killed in the battle or their mourning families, depending upon which version of the story you hear).

The third phenomenon most commonly told about VMI involves a ghoulish figure with sallow face and bleeding scar that has been dubbed "the Yellow Peril." What this thing is or how it relates to the history of the institution is somewhat unclear, but it has terrified cadets who have witnessed it, and has often been described as if it were seeking something.

With the exception of the Civil War years, cadets have walked picket posts during the school year, twenty-four hours a day, seven days a week, since the founding of the college. Many of the incidents of ghostly activity at the college have been reported by cadets on guard duty, and the long, lonely nighttime hours of such patrols have certainly contributed to what people have seen over the years.

Ghost stories are, in fact, "a favorite topic of cadets," according to Colonel Keith E. Gibson, VMI's director of museum operations. "When study is over, they begin to conjure up their own stories of ghosts at the institute."

"Jackson Memorial Hall lays claim to two ghosts—if there are in fact ghosts at VMI. The hall is named, of course, after the celebrated Stonewall Jackson, and is also the location of one cadet suicide. That was in the 1960s, and is the stuff of which ghost stories tend to be made. Cadets vaguely know that story and the parts they don't know they fill in anyway. That's the nature of these things. Interestingly, there are very few *specific* stories that have been passed down in cadet lore." He did mention one, however, that we had not read about prior to our visit.

"There are always the suspicions that Little Sorrell, Jackson's horse, is a ghost at VMI," Gibson said, and that the mounted hide of the horse "comes alive here in the museum. Perhaps it's true, but I have been here at all hours of the night and morning, and I've never actually witnessed that." The horse itself is not stuffed and its remains, other than its hide, are buried on the grounds of the VMI campus.

Signs of construction were evident during our visit, the most obvious project underway being a new block of barracks that will replace the ones built in the 1940s and eventually house up to 1,500 cadets. Other improvements currently being made to the 169-year-old campus include renovations to all the academic buildings and the construction of a VMI Center for Leadership and Ethics.

Most of the cadets had already gone home for the summer when we visited VMI in May 2008, and many of those still there were in the process of heading out, so the campus was

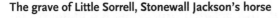

The grave of Little Sorrell, Stonewall Jackson's horse

not crowded. We were shown around by Dominique Baker, the cadet in charge of campus tours, who was staying at VMI for the summer semester between her junior and senior years. Like most of its students, she has herself sensed some strange things at the school and heard any number of related stories which, she said, tend to assume a very individualistic nature.

"If you stop any cadet and say, 'Tell me a VMI ghost story,' I guarantee you will not be told the same story twice," she said. One thing many of them have in common, however, is where they take place.

"Most of the ghost stories I've heard have been set in the barracks," Baker told us. "When you're a Rat (i.e., a freshman), you have to live on the fourth floor, and you run up and down the stairs all day long. Every year you get to move down a floor and the first classmen live on the bottom floor. The fifth level, where you can see the turrets," are where many ghostly phenomena have been reported and where cadets are rumored to have disappeared.

Baker also pointed out the lamp posts surrounding the barracks, which have also been the focus of stories and spectral sightings.

"I call them 'suicide lamps,'" she said. "Apparently, sometimes after cadets would get drummed out for honor violations, instead of just continuing with their lives, which would have been awful anyway, they would hang themselves on these lamps. Last year, I was lucky enough to have one right outside my window."

While most of what she has personally encountered has been relatively innocuous, and taken the form of things like doors inexplicably flying open, Baker does not question the essential basis of the various stories.

"Obviously, we do think the barracks is haunted to the max, because so many people have killed themselves there," she said. "It's creepy and I know it's haunted. There's no doubt about it."

While some might think that construction of a new block of

barracks might allow the cadets to finally live in a nonhaunted environment, that is not likely, and the seeds of ghost stories associated with it have already been sown.

"Unfortunately, one of our construction workers died there," Baker said, and this has unnerved some of the cadets. Her roommate from last year, she said, is adamant about never living in the unfinished Third Barracks, which she maintains are already haunted.

To prove to us that every cadet has their own ghost stories, Baker stopped almost every cadet we passed and asked what they knew about the campus's haunted legacy. We were regaled with numerous variations on the basic stories we had been hearing about the place.

One cadet, for example, gave an account of something that happened to a friend during his freshman year when he was on a guard detail that required him to periodically check on one of the cannons set up outside the barracks.

"He came out to check it and saw somebody in a Civil War uniform," cadet Jordan Combs told us. "He thought it was a reenactor, so he yelled at him to see what he was doing, and the guy took off running." The cadet followed the uniformed figure between two buildings toward a wood line, just feet behind him the whole way. And as soon as they entered the trees, the mysterious figure simply disappeared.

Colonel Gibson is somewhat philosophical—and very diplomatic—in his attitudes about whether or not the VMI campus is haunted. Despite the vast amount of ghostly lore that has been generated about VMI, he said that he does not believe the campus is haunted *per se*.

"I think that there is a great spirit that resides over the institute," he said. "Whether it takes the form of a ghostly presence is not clear. But I think that members of the cadet corps definitely have a sense that they are in a place where great things have happened and there is thus an atmosphere about it."

CHAPTER 26

Ghosts of the Valley
WINCHESTER

In Winchester, the oldest city west of the Blue Ridge Mountains, spirits abound. It is a strange mixture from the spirit world; heroes who fought in the War for Southern Independence as well as from the American Revolution, to those spirits who are still with us for reasons known only to themselves.

—Mac Rutherford, *Historic Haunts of Winchester*

WINCHESTER MAY VERY WELL BE the most densely haunted city in the entire Commonwealth of Virginia. While I don't have any statistical data to support that suspicion, I did hear more credible firsthand accounts of ghostly presences there than anywhere else I visited while working on this book—and had some personal experiences of my own to reinforce them.

Located at the north end of the Shenandoah Valley, Winchester is the northernmost community of any size in the state; little more than hills, forest, and a few hamlets can be found in the fifteen or twenty miles between it and the West Virginia state line to the west and the Maryland line to the north. It is an old town, its first non-native settlers arriving in 1729, and is the earliest city in the state to have been established west of the Blue Ridge Mountains. That fact alone can go a long way toward explaining its apparently high incidence of hauntings.

Winchester is somewhat off the beaten track, at least when compared to more traditional tourist destinations like Williamsburg, and it has far fewer published accounts of haunted venues than does that Colonial-era city. By all accounts, however, the city of about twenty-five thousand living residents has scores of haunted sites and virtually every historic building along its Old Town Pedestrian Mall is reputed to have one or more ghosts residing in it.

My wife and I spent the better part of three days investigating a number of the purportedly haunted sites in and around the historic city.

FRIDAY
We began our ghosthunting expedition in Winchester at the historic Fuller House Inn, a bed-and-breakfast that is itself reputed to be haunted, where we spent the last weekend in April 2008. While the main part of the sprawling, three-story house was

constructed in 1854 and incorporates elements of the Federal
and Greek Revival architectural styles, its oldest portions date to
1780 and were built as servant quarters for a plantation that was
once located near the site. A later, Italianate-style section was
added sometime after the Civil War.

Namesake for the inn is Dr. William McPherson Fuller, a
prominent dentist from Gettysburg, Pennsylvania, who purchased the property in 1859 around the time he was married
and in anticipation of needing a larger home for his family. (His
original, smaller house, on nearby Braddock Street, was used by
Confederate General Stonewall Jackson as a headquarters during the Civil War and is now operated as a museum.) He raised
his family in the home and dwelled there until his death in 1913
at the age of eighty-seven.

Proprietor Debby Johnson and her husband Richie Oram
have lived in the Fuller House for more than a decade, and turned
it into Winchester's first bed-and-breakfast in 2002. While both
of them have had numerous ghostly experiences in Winchester,
neither have had any in their own house. Many other people
they know have, however, including Debby's daughter Avery,
Richie's sister Lindy, a psychic friend, and numerous guests. In
particular, people have seen the specter of a soldier in some sort
of historic uniform standing on the stairway next to the room in
which we were staying.

After checking in at the Fuller House Inn, Debby gave us a
ride down to the historic center of town in the traditional Lon-
don cab she and Richie use and, once there, gave us an overview
of the downtown.

Debby then showed us around a restaurant called the Village Square that is in a haunted building she used to own and
where she had a number of paranormal experiences. We chatted a little bit with the bartender, Ted, who confirmed that weird
things do tend to happen in the building.

"One time, I was walking past the Tea Room," Ted said, describing one of the rooms toward the back of the restaurant, in its oldest section. Out of the corner of his eye, he saw "a big white object," which he assumed was Dan, the restaurant's white-clad chef. When he reached the kitchen, however, he discovered Dan there, which prompted him to go straight back to the Tea Room to see what had caught his eye. Nothing was there, and even now, he said, it sends shivers up his spine to think about it.

Ted also mentioned a door to the basement that is supposed to remain unlocked when the restaurant is open and locked when the establishment is closed, but which will become relocked for no apparent reason when the staff is working. And in the area called the Piano Room, there is an ongoing problem with flickering lights, even though an electrician has repeatedly inspected the wiring and confirmed that there is nothing wrong with it.

Cork Street Tavern

Our next stop was the Cork Street Tavern, which is in an antebellum building, one block off the city's pedestrian zone, which includes among its claims to fame being shelled during the Civil War. More pertinent to us were rumors we had heard about a ghost that lurks about a particular table and trips people walking past it! We asked to sit at the haunted table when we went in and were duly escorted to it.

The first person we chatted with was our waitress, Sharon, who told us that the area around the table is indeed haunted by the spirit of a man that regularly trips the waitresses—herself included—and female guests (Diane was very careful while maneuvering around the table and did not suffer any mishaps). We learned a little while later that this had happened to a customer as recently as the day before.

Sharon said a number of other spirits are believed to haunt the establishment, including that of a woman who sits near one of the windows and calls out the name "John." (We later learned that an owner of one of the homes that now comprise the Cork Street Tavern was named John, as was a co-owner of the first restaurant on the site, John Hoffman, either of which might be relevant to the manifestation in question.)

Current owner Joel Smith chatted with us for a few minutes about the lore associated with his restaurant.

"It's haunted," was the first thing he said to us of his establishment, which he has run since 1985. "Over the years, I have easily witnessed 150 to 200 different incidents" of a paranormal nature.

Joel went on to explain to us that what is now the Cork Street Tavern was originally two different Federal-style homes built in the 1820s, and that the area we were sitting in had actually been the alley between them. The buildings were unified probably around the 1880s, after which they housed a succession of businesses, including a feed store and an African-American

Baptist church from about 1900, and became a restaurant for the first time in 1932. It expanded its operations in the 1960s, purchasing adjacent property that is now the kitchen of the current establishment, and continued to operate up through the early 1970s. Several owners ran it over the following decade, and it finally went out of business in 1983, after which the building was almost completely gutted.

Joel and a number of business partners acquired the building and some adjacent property and, after thoroughly renovating it, opened the Cork Street Tavern in 1985.

"We used to have a fair amount of things happen in here," Joel said. "Two or three of us would be sitting around late at night after everything was closed having a late meal. The outside door would be locked, but we'd hear that inside foyer door creak open, and we would hear footsteps." The steps would then come right up to a point nearby and then stop. "And there were a lot of times when it sounded like people were eating, plates clanking, that sort of thing."

"I've probably had more happen here than anybody else," Joel said. "Maybe because I'm the sole surviving original owner. There were almost half a dozen of us originally. And I'm here at all hours, twenty-four hours a day." Joel lives in an apartment above the restaurant.

"When you are lying in bed at one o'clock in the morning, and all of a sudden all the lights in the building suddenly turn on, you kind of freak out," he said. "Okay, I can understand light going out, but all the lights coming on—what the heck! That's something that continues to this day."

Other experiences Joel has had include seeing a tall man in dark formal clothes with a top hat walking past open doors of the room he has been in while otherwise alone in the building. He had just woken up the first time it happened.

"I jumped out of bed and ran out in the hall to see who the

heck was in my apartment," he said. "But there was nobody there."

He said several other people working in the building have had similar experiences, including a dishwasher who also saw the dark-clothed man walking from one part of the building to another. Based on his investigation into the history of the place, Joel's theory is that the man might be John Hoffman, the owner of the original restaurant on the site. Part of his reasoning for this is the spectral female voice we had heard about from our waitress that, in addition to humming or singing indistinctly, he and many other people have heard calling out the name "John."

Joel said as much as six months might go by without anything paranormal happening, but then several things will happen in a short period of time, as had been the case recently. For better or worse, we did not see anything while we were there.

Once we had finished up at the Cork Street Tavern, we headed back to the Fuller House Inn, rested a little, and then got ready for the evening. We had hit it off pretty quickly with Debby and Richie, and the four of us spent the evening drinking, dining out, and chatting about the haunted history of Winchester and the Fuller House Inn.

SATURDAY

We started the day with a fortifying English breakfast courtesy of Richie, who was experimenting with menus for the pub he was getting ready to open in the fall of 2008. We then headed out to spend the day investigating a number of sites in and around the vicinity of Winchester, including Mount Hebron Cemetery, Belle Grove Plantation, Cedar Creek Battlefield, and the Wayside Inn (the latter three of which have their own chapters devoted to them in this book).

Mount Hebron Cemetery

We had decided to eat that evening at the Village Square and, after resting up a little in the early evening, headed over there for dinner. Half of what is now the restaurant was once owned by Debby Johnson, our hostess in Winchester, and run as an antique shop called Stone Soup. She had told us about a number of really weird things that had happened to her and others while she was there, including sightings of a spectral young woman in archaic attire, spots of extremely cold air, and the heavy tread of ghostly bootsteps headed toward Indian Alley, the narrow thoroughfare that runs behind the buildings on the west side of the Loudon Street pedestrian zone.

One of the most profound and mysterious episodes at the site involved a Miami-based writer named David Salway, who Debby allowed to spend the night at the shop while he was working on a book about haunted sites in the 1990s.

"He slept downstairs in one of those two older rooms," she said, referring to the original portion of the shop. "He had a

sighting, and he was so flipped out" that he went home immediately and decided not to finish writing his book. Debby never
learned exactly what he had witnessed that had shaken him
so badly.

Debby also told us that Richie had had some strange experiences in the shop, which included hearing his name called
when no one else was there and feeling a cold presence pass
through him.

Ghosts did not harass us during our evening at the Village Square and, while we were enjoying an excellent meal, co-
owner David Smith sat with us for awhile and chatted about
the haunted history of his restaurant. It is located in what was
originally two different buildings, and had been opened in just
one of them about five years earlier.

When David and his partner Joerg Eichmann decided to
expand their operations, they purchased the adjoining building,
which at that point was being used for Debby's antique shop,
and had previously served a number of different functions since
the 19th century, including a drugstore that ran a speakeasy in
a hidden basement during Prohibition. We were actually eating
in one of the two oldest rooms in the building—by all accounts
the most haunted ones—near the back of the restaurant, and
the trapdoor leading into the basement was evident nearby (this
subterranean area is popular with ghosthunters, who like to
spend the night in it).

David was averse to using the word "haunted" to describe
the spectral inhabitants of the property, and preferred to say that
"there are others living here besides human beings. There are
ghosts living here."

"We do know that there is a mother, Jeanelle, and her little
girl," David told us. "For the most part, they were over here,
and we never really had much of anything over on the other
side until we expanded." After the two buildings were unified,

however, the ghosts—especially that of the little girl—started to become active in areas where they had not been previously been noticed.

"She can be a little bit mischievous—things like knocking glasses off of counters," David said of the child. "So, the staff knows not to set glasses too close to the edge of the counters, where she can reach up and get them." He said glasses have even flown off tables at which guests were sitting and that this has scared some of them.

Most of the restaurant staff members cope pretty well with working in a haunted establishment. A few years ago, however, one of them, a man from Mexico, reacted very badly to his discovery that the place was haunted, and had some sort of a nervous breakdown. Some of his relatives ultimately had to remove him from the room above the restaurant where he had been living and put him on a plane back to his homeland.

After finishing up at the Village Square, Diane and I wandered back to our lodgings, stopping briefly near the tomb of Lord Fairfax, namesake of the county we live in, who is buried in the churchyard of the Christ Episcopal Church. His phantom is reported to have been seen here but did not manifest during the few minutes we were there.

Back at the Fuller House Inn, Diane passed out, and, mustering my second wind, I got ready to conduct what paranormal investigator Carl Kolchak liked to call a "midnight interview."

Debby had mentioned that other people had sensed a ghostly presence in her creepy, cluttered, 18th-century basement, so I figured that would be a good place to hang out for awhile, get some pictures, and see if anything turned up. So, between eleven o'clock and midnight I headed downstairs with my camera and tripod and started shooting images. It was definitely eerie, with crumbling masonry, big patches of orange mold, and some sort of old coal bunker that looked like it would be ideal for dissolving bodies in acid. I kept looking over my shoulder the whole time I was down there, half expecting some horrible thing to pop out from some shadowy corner and pounce on me.

SUNDAY

It was not until I went back upstairs, downloaded my photos, and started to peruse them that I found something tangible to unnerve me. There, peering out at me from a photo of a mirror I had taken, was a misshapen, spectral face, with large hollow eyes and open mouth!

I knew I needed to go back into the basement for a closer look at that mirror in order to help determine whether what I was looking at was likely paranormal in some way. I woke Diane up, showed her the picture, and asked if she wanted to accompany me. She wasn't having it. So, I headed back downstairs, found Richie, and showed the image to him, explaining that I really didn't want to go back into the basement alone. He was up for it, so we ventured into the basement.

What we found upon examination of the mirror was an odd dust pattern that produced the effect of a face. It is certainly conceivable that some paranormal force formed it into this pattern, but probably more likely that it did not, and in any event what the camera had picked up was not some ghostly face.

Richie and I retired to the room at the inn that he has transformed into a tiny facsimile of an English pub, and he told me about the full-sized pub—the Union Jack—he was at that time building in a historic building on the pedestrian mall. The property he had acquired for it was the old Union Bank, a building unique in Winchester because of its cast-iron façade. The lower two levels of the building had most recently been used as a jewelry store, and the third level had simply been sealed off. It had a somewhat shadowy past that involved rumors of a dishonest bank manager in the 1930s being caught embezzling and, as a consequence, blowing his brains out on the premises. Because of this, at least in part, the property had a reputation for being haunted.

"Do you want to check it out?" Richie asked me around 1:30 A.M. as we sipped our vodkas and orange juice.

"Sure!" I said. We had one more drink as we collected our cameras, tripods, flashlights, and other equipment and tossed it into Richie's truck. Then we headed off for Indian Alley and the rear entrance to the bank building.

Temporary lighting illuminated the inside of the building, which was gutted and under construction. We spent about an hour in the place, with Richie filling me in on what various areas had been used for and how he was transforming them, a particular point of pride being the fifty-foot wood bar he planned to install. The place consisted of a ground floor that ran the distance from Loudon Street at its front entrance to Indian Alley at its rear; a small second level that gave most of the first level a two-story ceiling; a third level maybe three quarters as long as the ground level; and a long, low, irregularly shaped cellar.

I took more than one hundred pictures, with particular emphasis on the small, second-level area, which Richie said had been the bank manager's office and was thus probably where he had committed suicide. I also got a picture of Richie there, looking westward out the back window of the building toward Indian Alley, over which a full moon had risen. The cellar was especially grim, with a damp, uneven floor and a ceiling too low for even a couple of relatively short men to stand upright. Richie said he planned to dig it out, and I wondered what he might end up finding underneath the dirt and rubble when he did.

We headed back to the Fuller Street Inn, mixed up a couple of Bloody Marys, and downloaded our photos. We started by running through them quickly, paying special attention to the images I had taken on the second level, to see if anything jumped out at us. Something did, but it wasn't from the second level.

On one of the shots I had taken on the third floor, we could see a large, distinct, blue-green orb high up in the center section of the three-pane window that dominated the end of the room facing onto Loudon Street.

"Is that the moon?" Richie asked me.

"No!" I said, scrolling over to the image I had taken of him a few minutes before the one we were looking at, which showed the moon outside the window to the west. Loudon Street, however, was exactly 180 degrees opposite, to the east. And, the directional limitations aside, the height of the building across the street meant that the moon would have been appearing in front of it, which obviously wasn't possible.

Closer examination of the photos revealed two sequential images shot from the second level up the stairs into the third in which faint orbs could be discerned, one higher than the other, as if it had been drifting slowly upward when I took the images. Two more images, these taken in the basement, revealed numerous pale gray orbs, floating in the air like spectral jellyfish. One of the images was one that Richie had taken of me, crouching in the damp cellar, the spheres clustering around me.

Rumors that the old Union Bank building was haunted were, apparently, correct.

Dawn was not far off when I stumbled back up to our room and collapsed into bed. It was not too many hours later that Diane woke me and told me Richie was up and cooking breakfast. Impressive. I got up, threw on some clothes, and headed downstairs for some coffee. Though I'm not much of a breakfast person, ghosthunting in the middle of the night really does seem to burn a large amount of energy, and I tucked into

Richie's delicious English breakfast, complete with fried tomato, with enthusiasm.

Richie and I shared our experiences of the night before with Debby and Diane, discussed the profound evidence of haunting we had found, and mulled over the implications that the ghostly presences might have on his pub. We decided at that point that we would need to return to Winchester once it was open and continue our investigation of the site.

Diane and I left Winchester exhausted and with the sense that it really was a town where a great number of spirits dwell side by side with the living. We were also pleased to have had such a productive visit and made such good new friends. And, while we were satisfied with the results of the ghosthunting we had done for the time being, we also knew that this old and haunted place warranted a much deeper investigation.

CHAPTER 27

Wayside Inn
MIDDLETOWN

Guests and hotel workers alike ... have reported seeing the ghostly images of Civil War veterans "milling around" in the lobby on occasion.

—L. B. Taylor Jr., "Non-Paying
Guests at the Wayside Inn"

SINCE 1797, THE WAYSIDE INN has provided food, drink, and lodging to travelers through the Shenandoah Valley, a fact that has allowed it to claim to be "the oldest continuously operating inn in America." This venerable institution is located in Middletown, a small, community with a current population of somewhat more than one thousand souls and is located about fourteen miles southwest of Winchester and thirteen northwest of Front Royal.

Middletown was ground zero for much of the savage combat that took place in the Shenandoah Valley during the Civil War, and is just a few miles from the Cedar Creek Battlefield. The proprietors of the Wayside Inn managed to cater to both sides during the war, however, and—by diplomatically offering hospitality to blue and gray alike—they managed to avoid being destroyed by either of the opposing armies, like so many other homes and businesses in the embattled valley.

This neutrality and modicum of safety maintained by the inn did not prevent fighting from sweeping into the town on more than one occasion, and soldiers were cut down on the Valley Pike right in front of the establishment. Some of them were buried on the grounds of the inn and their bodies remain interred there to this day, a number of markers attesting to this grim fact.

The history of the Wayside Inn significantly predates that of the Civil War, of course, and goes right back to the Colonial era, being founded just fourteen years after the end of the American Revolution. It was located right on the "Old Wagon Road," a thoroughfare through the valley that had been used as long as anyone could remember. Business picked up substantially when the inn was made a stagecoach stop and relay station for horses on the Valley Pike, an improved, ninety-three-mile-long highway started in 1834 that ran southwest from Winchester to Staunton and was supported by toll booths every five miles. (It is today known as U.S. Highway 11 and is no longer a toll road, most travelers preferring the parallel Interstate 81 anyway.)

After the Civil War, the Wayside Inn continued to provide hospitality to travelers, and in the early part of the 20th century the inn expanded and prospered in response to automobile traffic through the Shenandoah Valley.

In the 1960s, a financier and antique collector from Washington, D.C., thoroughly renovated, refurbished, and redecorated the inn and reinstated much of the 18th-century atmosphere that is now associated with it. Much of this was undone in 1985, when a devastating fire nearly gutted the establishment. Through great effort and dedication, however, it was restored and remains today a comfortable place for travelers.

My wife, Diane, had not availed herself of the substantial hot breakfast our host Richie had generously cooked for us that morning at the Fuller House Inn in Winchester, where we had spent the previous night, and had been warbling about hunger since we exited the interstate at Middletown. I was not yet overly hungry but we had been planning on visiting the Wayside Inn anyway, so after a quick reconnoitering drive from one end of town to the other, I flipped a U and headed back to it. By the time we got there, there was no question of her waiting in the car, and we went straight in for a bite.

I was pleasantly surprised to find the dining room sumptuously appointed with antiques and period-looking furniture, the wait staff attired in Colonial-style garb, and the menu replete with delicacies of the sort more often associated with faraway Williamsburg ("authentic regional American cuisine" in the words of the establishment). Among other things, these included spoon bread, country ham, and a variety of game, seafood, and desserts. I kept it simple and ordered a bowl of the peanut soup, a specialty of the Old Dominion since its earliest days that is a favorite of mine, while my wife ordered a more substantial club sandwich accompanied by some coleslaw she found especially agreeable.

Sustenance taken care of, we turned to the task at hand, namely getting a sense for whether or not the Wayside Inn was actually haunted. I had read a number of ghost stories associated with the inn, most of them related to its role in the Civil War, the many soldiers who had passed through the doors during the conflict, and those who had been slain and were buried nearby. Much of this lore involved sightings, by both staff and guests, of spectral soldiers in or around the inn.

While the managers of some establishments try to control what their subordinates say about such things, we discovered that was most assuredly not the case at the Wayside Inn. Indeed, everyone we talked with there was immediately and cheerfully forthcoming about their own experiences with and knowledge about its apparently haunted nature.

The first person we talked to was our waitress, Sandy, who, like the other women working in the dining room, was dressed in 18th-century-style garb, complete with mob cap. As soon as we identified ourselves and explained our mission, she mentioned that another group of ghosthunters had recently been at the inn and conducted an investigation in one of its older rooms, something we were hearing increasingly at the places we visited.

Sandy confirmed that many people consider the Wayside Inn to be haunted, confirmed that she herself believed it to be so, and noted that she had heard many accounts from other employees and guests to support this. She also said she has personally had some strange experiences in the two years she had worked at the inn and recounted a few of them to us.

"See the leaf on this table?" she asked, indicating a hinged extension on the table at which we were sitting. "As long as I've been here it's been up, it's never been down, because it's a wooden leaf and it's hard to get down."

"I was in here one day—and, as a matter of fact, one of the other girls was working with me—and I had just wiped this table off" and then went off to continue cleaning up elsewhere in the dining room, she said. Then, when she "came back to set

This dining room used to be the "old servant kitchen" and is
believed to be one of the most haunted sections of the Wayside Inn.

up [the table], the leaf was down. It can go down, but it's very,
very hard" and, furthermore, has a locking mechanism to keep
it in place. She was, naturally, spooked by the episode, and asked
the other woman working then if she knew anything about it,
but she said she did not. With some difficulty, she managed to
pull the obstinate leaf back up and then set the table.

We continued to munch our authentic regional fare at the
haunted table (or the table in the haunted dining room, whatever
the case might have been), and before long Sandy came back
with Anna, nicknamed "Grandma," a member of the housekeeping staff who had worked at the inn for more than twelve years.

Anna affirmed her belief that the inn was home to ghosts
and told us about a number of episodes that she and her coworkers had experienced while working at the inn. For her, these had
included passing through areas of very cold air in the hotel.

"You can just feel like something's around you," she said,
and that it does not feel like just cold air. She also said that one

of the young women she worked with had sometimes heard a baby crying in the "old slave kitchen," an area now used as a dining room that had once been used by slaves as a kitchen and was supposed to be among the earliest original sections of the inn.

Our lunch finished, we decided to explore the sprawling historic inn, the areas of which include seven antique-filled dining rooms with names like the Lord Fairfax Room, the Portrait Dining Room, and the Old Servant Kitchen (aka, the "old slave kitchen"). Our waitress, Sandy, appeared while we were looking around and led us to the latter, a small, dark, completely enclosed, wood-paneled dining area filled with many original furnishings. We found this little room to be especially interesting based on its appearance alone, and it was easy to see why it has had a number of ghostly incidents associated with it over the years. We spent about fifteen minutes there, poking around and taking pictures and, while we didn't see anything out of the ordinary, it would be fair to say that we could easily imagine the presence of lingering spirits there.

The last person we talked to during our visit was Hannah, the young woman working at the front desk of the inn. Right off she mentioned—echoing a theme that was recurring for us during on our trip to the Shenandoah Valley in particular—that a number of previous groups of ghosthunters had visited the inn in the recent past. She noted that one in particular had visited the previous Halloween and had conducted a séance in one of the guest rooms upstairs.

While she had not personally experienced any ghostly episodes at the inn—attributing this to the fact that she worked days and not nights—she, too, expressed her belief that the inn is haunted. Part of what convinced her of this, she said, was not just the many episodes she had heard from other people who had experienced weird things at the Wayside Inn, but that many of them experienced the same sorts of things.

One such episode she recounted to us involved a lady who has been coming to stay at the Wayside Inn for the past five years. During her most recent trip, she became distraught after feeling something invisible brush against her while she was alone in her room.

Besides passing on to us some of the establishment's ghost lore, Hannah also very accommodatingly gave us the keys to the inn's two oldest rooms—appropriately named one and two—so that we could take a look at them and snap a few ghosthunting photos.

No ghost orbs or anything else out of the ordinary turned up in the photos we took and—other than the sense that something certainly could have been present in the old slave kitchen—we didn't personally sense or experience anything distinct or specific at the Wayside Inn that would have suggested it was occupied by spirits. One thing, however, is for sure: every one of the people who worked there that we talked to claimed to be convinced that it was indeed haunted, and that has got to count for something.

DISTRICT OF COLUMBIA

Washington
    America's Greatest Haunted City
    Ford's Theatre
    Decatur House

CHAPTER 28

America's Greatest Haunted City

WASHINGTON

If there is a common denominator to these Washington ghosts, it is one of near-European romanticism and a degree of intrigue and mystic involvement that you will never find in other cities in America.

—Hans Holzer, *The Ghosts That Walk in Washington*

AN OVERVIEW OF HAUNTED SITES in the nation's capital reveals it to be a city rife with ghosts and places where inexplicable events have been known to occur. In fact, if you search long enough, you will discover that practically the whole city is haunted, and that the unresolved business of more than two centuries has bound within it an uncanny number of ghosts. Those who work in the city rush past dozens of possibly haunted places every single day, most of them oblivious to the uneasy spirits who dwell there. But Washington, D.C., most certainly is, as the now-defunct *Washington Star* newspaper wrote in 1891, "America's greatest haunted city."

I have lived in the Washington area about two decades altogether, worked or conducted business there over the years, and have heard many stories of ghostly phenomena associated with it.

"There is ... a general acceptance of the occult" in Washington, psychic researcher Hans Holzer wrote in 1971, suggesting that it may be "because the business of government in itself is, by its very uncertainty, prone to cause a certain curiosity for knowledge beyond the five senses." To whatever extent that was true nearly four decades ago, it appears to be much less so today, and neither openmindedness nor a sense of humor seem to be traits associated with the directors of possibly haunted historic and governmental sites in or around the nation's capital.

Many parts of Washington are also less accessible today than they were prior to September 11, 2001, and the uneasy spirit of that day persists in the city as palpably as any ghost. In the downtown area in particular, where a great many government buildings are located, a number of streets have been closed to vehicular traffic and nearly all of them are lined with Jersey barriers and huge, car-bomb-proof concrete planters. Ghosthunters will now find that security requirements have made it much more complicated to get into the White House, the Capitol, or any number of other high-profile sites.

All of that said, there are still many enticements for ghosthunters in Washington, D.C. This book is concerned only with sites that are both believed by many to be haunted and are also publicly accessible. It furthermore concentrates on sites with some historical merit that are in areas that are most easily and safely visited.

Beyond readily visited sites in the safer sections of the city, there are also throughout the District innumerable places that are believed to be haunted but which are closed to the public, either because they are on private property or within restricted government facilities. Ghosthunters affiliated with the military or other government agencies might have access to reputedly haunted places like Fort McNair—where those convicted of conspiring to assassinate Lincoln were confined and four of them were subsequently executed—or St. Elizabeth's Hospital, half of which has been taken over in recent years by, of all things, the Department of Homeland Security.

Two particularly interesting publicly accessible sites are the Decatur House and Ford's Theatre, both located in D.C. Northwest, and each with a chapter devoted to it in this book. A number of other significant purportedly haunted sites are described more briefly on the following pages of this chapter.

Ghostly phenomena begin at the geographical center of the city—on Capitol Hill—and radiate out from it. Many are associated with the Northwest quarter of the city, which we will venture into after exploring the Hill a bit.

Numerous ghost stories have been associated with the Capitol building itself over the years and it is widely believed, by those inclined to believe such things, to be haunted. Indeed, if conflict, strong emotions, and unresolved issues are among the basis for ghostly phenomena, then it certainly makes sense that it would be. Phenomena people have reported over the years have included seeing figures animate and move about in Statuary Hall; a variety of ghosts—including people purported to have been killed in the building and the ubiquitous Civil War soldiers—throughout the building, especially the Rotunda; and a black cat that is supposed to appear in the basement just before a national disaster occurs (e.g., the 1929 stock market crash, the 1963 Kennedy assassination).

Just to the northeast of the Capitol is the Supreme Court building, located at the site of the Old Brick Capitol. That long-gone structure was used by Congress for five years after British troops burned the Capitol in 1814, after which it subsequently served first as apartments, then as a Union prison during the Civil War, and finally as headquarters of the National Woman's Party, before being torn down in the 1930s to make way for the current building. By virtue of the Supreme Court's location on the site of the earlier building, it is rumored to be haunted by a number of ghosts. These include career politician John C. Calhoun, who dwelled in the building while serving in Congress and dreading the prospect of the coming Civil War; Confederate spy Belle Boyd, confined in the prison during the war; Henry Wirtz, commandant of the notorious Confederate prison at Andersonville, Georgia, who was hanged in the prison courtyard; and various other unnamed prisoners and guards.

Another reputedly haunted site on Capitol Hill is the Library of Congress. Paranormal phenomena that have been reported in its labyrinthine stacks over the years have included inexplicable banging sounds and heavy exhibit cases moving on their own. One specific story, supposedly corroborated by library staff, involves a police officer who helps people lost in the stacks find their way out and then, before disappearing, tells them he was killed several years before.

Moving westward off the Hill along Pennsylvania Avenue will take the ghosthunter past various storied and ostensibly haunted locations (and, after about a half mile, within a block or so of Ford's Theatre). One of these is the National Theatre, at 13th and E Streets, which was built in the 1830s and is still a popular venue for live entertainment that my wife and I have attended a number of times over the years. We did not witness anything supernatural during our visits to the theatre, but have heard some of the legends surrounding it. One involves an actor who was supposedly slain by a jealous colleague and buried in

The National Theatre

the establishment's basement, which is strictly off limits to the public (this is sometimes cited as corroboration of the legend, despite the fact that such areas often have restricted access).

Just a block past the National Theatre on Pennsylvania Avenue is the Willard Hotel, a grand and historical edifice that has been rightfully called "the Residence of Presidents," and housed many executives prior to their moves to the nearby White House. (It has always been one of my favorite hotels anywhere and has a personal connection, having been designed by an ancestor. Many years ago, I had the pleasure of spending a weekend in its upper-story Woodrow Wilson suite, and can honestly say I felt the spirit of the city while I was there, if not any specific ghosts). Ulysses S. Grant was one of the luminaries who lived at the hotel and has subsequently been not so much seen in it again as detected in the lobby by the smell of the stogies that were an omnipresent element of both his life and death.

Two more blocks along Pennsylvania Avenue—which is closed to vehicle traffic soon after it passes by the Willard—will bring a visitor to the White House, likely the place with the greatest reputation for being haunted in the capital city. Foremost among the ghosts said to haunt the executive mansion is Abraham Lincoln, and those who claimed to have encountered his shade there include Queen Wilhemina of the Netherlands during a visit to Washington.

Other ghosts purported to have been seen in the White House include Abigail Adams, associated especially with the East Room, where she continues to hang laundry in death as she did in life; Dolly Madison, who is said to have appeared to gardeners, possibly in a perpetually annoyed response to Mrs. Woodrow Wilson having her prized rose bushes moved; and a spectral Redcoat arsonist from the War of 1812, who people have seen trying to set fire to the place with a phantasmal torch. And President Harry S. Truman on more than one occasion said he could sense the presence of his predecessors, especially those he believed had been handed messes not of their own making.

"While I work from early morning until late at night, it is a ghostly place. The floors pop and crack all night long," he wrote of the White House in his diary on January 6, 1947, going on to mention the specters of James Buchanan, Martin Van Buren, James Madison, and Andrew Johnson. "They all walk up and down the halls of this place and moan about what they should have done and didn't. ... So the tortured souls who were and are misrepresented in history are the ones who come back. It's a hell of a place."

Several houses across from the White House on Lafayette Park are also reputed to be haunted. These include the Decatur House, haunted by the spirit of a hero whose limitless ambitions were thwarted by an untimely death; and Blair House, where a shade believed by some to be that of Woodrow Wilson has been reported sitting in a rocking chair in one of the bedrooms (although Wilson's own home elsewhere in the city would seem to be a more appropriate haunt for his spirit).

Continuing a few blocks further west to 1799 New York Avenue N.W. will bring a ghosthunter to the Octagon, a truly strange residence, which despite its name is actually an irregularly shaped, three-story brick building that has just six sides but eight angles. It was designed by William Thornton, architect of the U.S. Capitol, and built between 1798 and 1800 for Colonel John Tayloe III, original owner of the Willard Hotel and possibly the wealthiest Virginia planter at the time. In 1814, Tayloe invited President James Madison and his wife, Dolly, to dwell at the house while the White House was being rebuilt after the War of 1812, and it was there that the president signed the Treaty of Ghent, which ended that war. Various ghosts have been reported in the house over the years—including Tayloe and a number of servants—and apparently linger on in connection with a series of strange tragedies that marked the home. One of these involved one of Tayloe's daughters, who was killed when she plummeted down the steps; her screams have been heard and the candle she carried seen by visitors to the place. Another involves a second daughter who, bizarrely, also pitched down the steps, breaking her neck and pushing up the carpet at the foot of the stairs when she plowed into it; that carpet is said to curl up as a result, despite the best efforts of people to keep it down.

A trip further westward through the district will eventually bring a visitor to Georgetown, once an independent town built along the banks of the Potomac (where Ninian Beall, another of my ancestors, owned significant tracts of property in the years prior to the Revolutionary War). It is one of the oldest and most characteristic sections of the city and site of numerous buildings with a longstanding reputation for being haunted.

One of the most famous of these is Halcyon House, a Georgian-style home located in the heart of Georgetown. It was built and occupied by Benjamin Stoddert, a merchant whose business failed from a lack of adequate attention during his service as Secretary of the Navy during President John Adams' administration. A subsequent owner renovated the home, and the changes to it are said to have angered the lingering spirit of Stoddert, who has been reported sitting in the location where his favorite chair once stood. Visitors have also reported waking up to discover themselves levitating a foot above the bed, seeing lights go on and off on their own, and discovering that an old woman has tucked into bed children who have stayed overnight in the house.

A number of other ostensibly haunted sites can be visited in D.C. Northwest alone. Beyond the famous Willard, for example, a number of other hotels throughout the city are reputed to be haunted.

One of these is the Shoreham—now owned by the Omni Hotel Corporation—which was built in 1930 and is located on upper Connecticut Avenue, at its intersection with Calvert Street. Not long after it opened, two young women were rumored to have died under circumstances both tragic and mysterious, and the rooms where it happened were shut up and used as storage areas for many years. They were eventually reopened and are widely known as the hotel's "Ghost Suite" as a result of the spirits people claim to have seen in them. Another is the Hay-Adams (at 800 16th Street N.W., on Lafayette Park), an Italian Renaissance-style luxury hotel built in 1928 on the sites of the former homes of John Hay and Henry Adams. The ghost most commonly associated with it is that of Adams' wife, Clover, who is believed to have committed suicide in their home and who has been seen or felt throughout the hotel. Other reported incidents at the Hay-Adams have included all the guest rooms on the second floor opening at one time, an inability to keep the housekeeping closet on the sixth floor locked, and the inexplicable scent of mimosa on the eighth floor.

Various abodes of the dead in Washington are also believed to be haunted, and the most prominent of these is Rock Creek Cemetery, an eighty-six-acre memorial park with a natural

Henry Adams House

rolling landscape that was established in 1719 (at Rock Creek Church Road and Webster Street, N.W.). One of the sites within it where some of the strangest phenomena have been reported is the Adams Memorial, where the aforementioned Clover Adams and her husband are buried. The statue before it, of a hooded androgynous figure, was crafted by premiere American sculptor Augustus Saint-Gaudens, who wordily dubbed it "The Mystery of the Hereafter and the Peace of God That Passeth Understanding." It is widely known by the shorter nickname "Grief," and people have reported both seeing it weep and cry uncontrollably while in its presence. Many other significant monuments are located in the cemetery, and it has been the site of many other supernatural occurrences as well.

There are many more haunted places in the District of Columbia and the sites described in this chapter represent just a handful of those that are publicly accessible. Suffice it to say, there are many, many more places of potential interest in the capital city for ghosthunters interested in investigating the phantasms and stories associated with them.

CHAPTER 29

Decatur House
WASHINGTON, D.C.

Oh, Lord, I'm a dead man!

—Stephen Decatur, March 21, 1820

STEPHEN DECATUR GAZED MOROSELY from the window of the second-floor drawing room of his house onto the leafless trees of Lafayette Square. He was uncharacteristically withdrawn, even brooding, according to the guests at the soiree his unwitting wife had hosted. He had concealed from her and, indeed, from even his closest friends that he had a rendezvous at Bladensburg dueling grounds in Maryland early the next morning. None suspected that by the same time the next day,

233

this greatest of all American naval heroes would be dead.

One year later, or so the legend goes, servants returning to the house spotted the face of Decatur at that window. Rumors of hauntings have been associated with the house ever since.

On March 20, 1978, 157 years after the servants' report, Vicki Sopher, director of the Decatur House, and a few of her staff, decided to test the legend, according to an article from that year in the *Washington Post*. Seated in the drawing room, they waited in eerie silence and candlelight for the ghost of Stephen Decatur to appear. It did not. Undeterred, Sopher vowed to try again the following year. If she had any success, I could find no record of it.

There was a second, more rigorous, attempt, a couple of years ago—this time by professional ghosthunters equipped with all the paraphernalia of the trade. Decatur House Assistant Director Katherine Malone-France was present for the investigation, and she informed me that, in spite of the meticulousness of the investigators, they failed to detect any sign of a ghostly presence.

Does this mean that the ghost of Stephen Decatur no longer haunts his home on Lafayette Square in Washington, D.C.? It is possible, but somehow I doubt it. What both these investigations had in common was that they focused on the drawing room and the events of the evening before the duel. They misread the man, I believe—and failed to take into account his iron will and ruthless ambition. The place to search for Decatur's ghost is on the ground floor of his home, in the room in which he died. And the time to look is not the evening of March 20, but rather the evening of March 21. That search, I propose, would not find Decatur staring distractedly at the trees of Lafayette Square, but, rather, would find him focused single-mindedly on the object of his ambitions: the White House.

It was with these thoughts in mind, that my wife and I approached the front entrance to the Decatur House on a cold clear afternoon in January 2008. We had just lunched at one of the several good Chinese restaurants in the District's Chinatown. It was a beautiful day to take in the sights of our nation's capital, so we decided to walk the several blocks to Pennsylvania Avenue.

I had completed my research into Stephen Decatur, and I had come to understand that his sights had been set much higher than the U.S. Navy. Understanding him, as I now believed I did, I felt it was most appropriate to approach the house from across Lafayette Square with the White House, gleaming now in the bright winter sun, at my back.

As I neared the front of the house that Decatur had built to further his ambitions and peered though the window into the room where he died, I was fully prepared, if not actually expecting, to see his ghostly apparition staring forlornly from that window through the leafless trees of Lafayette Square toward the object of his aspirations. To my chagrin, what I actually viewed was a table saw and workman's tools: the house was undergoing a thorough renovation, and the room was in total disarray. I was disappointed but still resolved. What ghost could make an appearance in such a setting?

To understand why I, who am actually a skeptic on the subject of ghosts, came to expect Decatur's presence, the reader must first understand the man and the role of the house that he built. Then it may be possible to see that it is sometimes not the house that is haunted, but the spot on which it rests.

THWARTED AMBITION

"Oh, Lord, I'm a dead man," Stephen Decatur groaned as he collapsed onto the cold bare earth of the Bladensburg dueling grounds.

His opponent's pistol ball had torn into his entrails, severing pelvic arteries. Blood soaked his fine wool pants. He would not live to see the next sunrise.

Eight paces away, his opponent, Commodore James Barron, also fell. But Barron was more fortunate. Decatur had aimed low—as indeed Barron had as well—to wound, not to kill, and his ball had struck Barron's hip bone and ricocheted down his thigh. Barron would always walk with a limp, but he would survive.

The U.S. Navy's most illustrious commander died that evening. He was only forty-one—killed by a man he had once described as "more than a father."

The nation mourned. Presidents paid their respects. His famously beautiful wife was inconsolable.

How had this come to pass? How had a man who had accomplished so much, had risen so quickly and was esteemed by so many, come to this end? And why, almost two centuries later, does one expect to see his ghost still haunting the home in which he died? What is the unfinished business that could tether this iron-willed man, this hero of the Barbary Coast and the War of 1812, to this mortal plane? How could this man, so noble in so many ways, become bound (and I would add, justly so) to a continuing earthly purgatory? Those questions are the ones that haunted me and that I will now seek to answer for the reader.

Decatur first burst onto the consciousness of his nation in 1804. It was a young nation and much in need of heroes. America was fed up with having her merchant ships preyed upon by the piratical Barbary States of the North African Coast. Rather than continue the ignominious practice of paying tribute, President Thomas Jefferson ordered the construction of warships that would sail to the shores of Tripoli and teach the pirates a lesson. Young Lieutenant Stephen Decatur sailed with that expedition.

Things quickly became complicated.

One of the newly minted American warships, the U.S. Navy frigate *Philadelphia*, through a combination of misfortune and bad judgment on the parts of her officers, had ran aground on a

sandbar while pursuing a smaller Tripolitan craft. She was subsequently captured, along with her crew, by the Pasha of Tripoli,
Yusuf Karamanli. His men succeeded in floating *Philadelphia*
off the sandbar and sailed her into Tripoli harbor. Unfortunately
for the U.S. Navy, the captured American frigate was now the
most powerful ship in the Tripolitan fleet—and she was protect-
ing the pasha from the very Americans who had sailed her to
the Barbary Coast to chastise him!

Fortunately for Decatur, however, the decision of *Philade-
phia's* commander to surrender her set the stage for the dashing young officer's leap to glory. Decatur was given the mission
of destroying *Philadelphia*. His stratagem was a combination of
cunning and daring, and employed a captured Barbary ketch,
rechristened *Intrepid*, so as not to alarm the Tripolitans. The
Americans on deck were disguised as Maltese sailors, and
below, crammed into the narrow confines of the hold, were seventy determined seaman and marines.

In what Horatio Nelson, England's greatest naval commander, called "the most bold and daring act of the age," Decatur was able to close on the unsuspecting *Philadelphia*. His crew
scrambled aboard, quickly subdued the Tripolitan crew, and put
Philadelphia to the torch. As *Intrepid* pulled away from the flam-
ing vessel, the Americans looked back at a floating inferno that
was drifting toward the pasha's castle. Her former commander,
looking down from his place of confinement, watched with
undoubtedly mixed emotions as she exploded dramatically at
the very foot of the castle walls.

At home, Decatur was a hero. He was promoted to captain
over lieutenants more senior to him, generating envy and resent-
ment among his peers—sentiments that would haunt him
throughout his career. Later, he would even be placed in com-
mand over the unfortunate commander who had surrendered
Philadelphia to the Tripolitans, Captain William Bainbridge.

This would have fatal repercussions for Decatur. Bainbridge, by providing this opportunity for heroism, was instrumental in launching Decatur's career—and was later a major player in bringing it to an end.

Decatur's career prospered, launched as it had been by his exploits against the Barbary Pirates and reinforced by subsequent achievements during the War of 1812, and was driven by an ambition that was at times ruthless. By 1820—the year of his death—Decatur was an influential member of the Board of Naval Commissioners in Washington, D.C. It was in this role that he came into final and fatal conflict with his former friend and mentor, Commodore James Barron.

In spite of being a capable naval officer, history will remember Barron not just for having fatally wounded Decatur, but also for having surrendered the U.S. frigate *Chesapeake* to the British ship *Leopard* in 1807. The incident was over four British deserters who had allegedly joined the American Navy and were thought by the British to be serving on the American ship. As *Chesapeake* had barely put up resistance, Commodore Barron was brought before a naval court martial. Decatur had the unfortunate duty of serving as a member of the board that found Barron guilty of one of the four charges brought against him, that he had neglected, "on the probability of an engagement, to clear his ship for action." His punishment: "Suspension from all commands without pay or official emoluments of any kind for the term of five years."

The end of that term found Barron in Copenhagen as the captain of an American merchant ship. The War of 1812 was raging and he was unable to immediately return to resume his service with the Navy; for reasons that remain somewhat unclear, Barron did not succeed in reaching Washington until early in 1819 to apply in person for an appointment to active service. He was referred to the Board of Naval Commissioners, of which Stephen Decatur was a member.

Decatur did not support Barron's return to active service. Barron's delay in returning to the United States was key to Decatur's position—but also quite possibly, was a more personal matter, a perceived and probably unintended slight from years past that Decatur could not bring himself to forgive. Historians surmise that it involved an unfortunate comment that Barron made concerning Decatur's wife, Susan Marbury, then his fiancée, who was one-eighth African-American. Whether that was the object of Barron's comment we will probably never know, but whatever it was, it poisoned their relationship thereafter.

In any event, lengthy correspondence ensued. Decatur, who was more concerned with his own aspirations than with Barron's, could not bring himself to give Barron what he craved possibly even more than reinstatement in the Navy—the restoration of Decatur's friendship and respect. The exchange, probably unintentionally on Decatur's part, only served to further provoke and humiliate Barron, which ultimately drove him to challenging Decatur to a duel. The result was a tragic and unnecessary end to what had once been a warm friendship.

Looking back on the fight and the events leading up to it, many, including Decatur's wife, concluded that it was the duelists' seconds who set events on their unwavering course and prevented any last-minute reconciliation. Decatur's second was none other than William Bainbridge, the unfortunate commander who had lost *Philadelphia* to the Tripolitans. In spite of a surface amicability, there was no love lost between Bainbridge and Decatur: Bainbridge had never overcome his jealousy and loss of self-esteem. As luck would have it, Barron's second also harbored issues. He was Jesse Elliot, a sworn enemy of Decatur's close friend, Oliver Hazard Perry.

The conditions that Bainbridge had arranged with Elliot were not those that Decatur had requested—and they made bloodshed inevitable. The weapons were pistols, the distance a mere eight paces. The opponents stood face-to-face.

"I shall give the order quickly," Bainbridge stated. "Present, one, two, three. You are neither to fire before the word *one*, nor after the word *three*."

"What could have induced you to do this act?" Decatur asked of Barron, as they both lay on the chill March ground.

Finally, now that it was too late, Decatur was appreciating the import of his indifferent words and choices that had seemed far less weighty at the time—at least to him but not, of course, to Barron. We can only surmise whether Decatur, in the brief time left to him, would also reexamine the role the duplicitous seconds had played in ensuring this bloody outcome.

As the opponents fell, both seconds, indifferent to the welfare of the combatants, vanished. Decatur was taken home by friends, to a loving wife who had no idea where he had gone when he had walked out of their house that cold morning. She only knew that when she awoke, he was gone. They brought him to a room to the left of the domed entrance hall, the room where he signed his will and then, a few hours later, died.

Behind Decatur's success was more than good fortune, more than audacity, and more than courage, although he had all three in abundance. What drove him was a reckless quest for glory that was rooted in a sometimes ruthless ambition.

Where this ambition was taking him can be seen in the location he chose for his house: Lafayette Square, across the street from the White House. It also can be seen in its design. Decatur used much of the fortune in prize money that he won during the War of 1812 to construct a home that would be, in his words, "suitable for foreign ministers and impressive entertainments." He selected as his architect none other than Benjamin Latrobe, the man who had designed the U.S. Capitol.

This house became a center of Washington social life, where

the dashing Decatur and his alluring wife entertained the capital's elite. In return, they were frequent guests of the Monroes at the White House.

That Decatur had aspirations of being more than just a guest in the White House is not attested to by his correspondence or other documentation. It has to be found in his actions and his relationships. But what else would one expect of the resourceful naval officer who had so successfully duped the Tripolitan prize crew on *Philadelphia*?

Could it be, in the leisure that death had provided, that Decatur looked back on the events leading up to the duel and could see how he and Barron—for whom he surely still harbored some affection—had been cleverly maneuvered into a duel by seconds who had no love for either of them? It is certainly easy to see how Decatur, cheated as he was of a possibly even more illustrious future, including, quite possibly, the highest office of the land, might not be able to just let go and move on. One need only think of the ambitious political candidates of our own era to get a sense of what it must have meant to Decatur, harboring his presidential dreams, to be cut off from life literally within sight of the White House—and then to die in a room whose sole window looked out at the object of his ambitions.

My wife and I entered the house from the rear, the main entrance now being closed. There was a docent sitting at a desk near the door, and I wasted little time in engaging her on the subject of ghosts. In what I have since come to learn would be a pattern, especially at the more established sites which are controlled by foundations or boards of governors, she referred me to Assistant Director Katherine Malone-France.

It was some weeks, however, before I succeeded in reaching Ms. Malone-France. She was rushed but, somewhat to my surprise, quite pleasant and forthcoming. She revealed to me her participation in the investigation a couple years previously and how it had yielded no indication of any other-worldly presence. She also told me that she had never received a credible report of ghostlike activity from her staff.

How is it then that stories persist of hauntings at the Decatur House, if not by Decatur himself then by his bereaved wife or even a denizen of the slave quarters behind the house? Are the stories groundless or were the investigations flawed? Did they fail to take into account the true nature of the man? Has the focus been on the wrong place and the wrong time?

I, for one, can see him plainly in my mind's eye, staring forlornly from his death-room toward the home he so desperately yearned for: the White House. I will return to the Decatur House some cold March evening, when the renovations in that room have been completed and the lights of the White House can be seen through the leafless trees of Lafayette Square—and Decatur, I believe, will be there.

CHAPTER 30

Ford's Theatre
WASHINGTON

It is required of every man ... that the spirit within him should walk abroad among his fellowmen, and travel far and wide; and if that spirit goes not forth in life, it is condemned to do so after death. It is doomed to wander through the world— oh, woe is me!—and witness what it cannot share, but might have shared on earth, and turned to happiness!

—Charles Dickens, *A Christmas Carol*

IN THE EARLY 1990S, my wife and I spent an evening between Christmas and New Year's Eve at Ford's Theatre, and during our time there we distinctly saw four separate ghosts and even learned their names. They were, in fact, the ghosts of Jacob Marley, Christmas Past, Christmas Present, and Christmas Future, and they were characters in a production of Charles Dickens' *A Christmas Carol*, which was an annual tradition at the historic theatre. But, beyond those thespian shades, we did not see or otherwise sense the presence of any lingering spirits.

I did, to be sure, encounter some particularly annoying ghosts of a modern nature prior to my visit to this famous theatre in Washington, D.C., in mid-April, 2008, but a bit more attention to detail, however, would probably have allowed me to avoid them. In short, while doing some online research prior to visiting Ford's Theatre, I stumbled across an outdated National Park Service Web page for the site that did not mention that "Ford's Theatre is currently undergoing a major renovation," as noted on the updated version of the page, which further notes that "the theatre will not be open for public access for several months" True, both versions of the page neglected to list the address for the theatre, but that seems like an overly subtle way of informing people they should not bother to visit it.

Upon actually venturing downtown to Ford's Theatre, I saw an old-fashioned, analog "Closed" sign hanging above the entrance that revealed the electronic specters that had deceived me into thinking it would be open until 5 P.M. A smaller sign revealed that it would not reopen until at least February 2009. Still, it was nice to be downtown with my other business dispensed with, the five-block walk from the new [Walter E.] Washington Convention Center had been nothing but pleasant, and the bright, sunny afternoon provided me with the perfect opportunity to take some decent pictures.

Dickensian spirits and Web clutter aside, the ghost com-

Ford's Theatre

monly associated with Ford's Theatre is, of course, Abraham
Lincoln, who was mortally wounded by assassin John Wilkes
Booth while attending a performance of *Our American Cousin*.
Ever since then, the small, historic theatre has been the site of
ongoing strange sightings and occurrences. The idea of Lincoln's
spirit haunting this theatre, however—or any other particular
spot, for that matter—is somewhat problematic.

For one thing, Lincoln had achieved many things of monu-
mentally historical significance during his terms of office and
must be ranked among our greatest presidents. Another argu-
ment against the presence of Lincoln's ghost at Ford's Theatre,
of course, is that it has been regularly spotted at so many other

places, including various locations in the White House and numerous sites in his home state of Illinois (described by John Kachuba in his own book, *Ghosthunting Illinois*). While it may be possible for a ghost to haunt several sites simultaneously, to travel back and forth between them, or even to have its essence parsed out to the various places with which he had connections in life, this would certainly be contrary to conventional wisdom associated with ghosts and their attributes.

Lincoln is, nonetheless, reputed to haunt Ford's Theatre, as is the spirit of John Wilkes Booth, the fanatically pro-Southern actor-turned-assassin who mortally wounded him with a shot to the head. Over the years, numerous people have claimed to see one or both of them in the theatre, typically in the raised box where they played out their ultimate drama. (The issue of the killer's specter is just as problematic as that of the slain president's in its own way, as Booth could hardly have succeeded in wreaking more damage to the Union than he did. A reasonable suggestion might be that he is tethered to this plane by deep regret for the grief his actions contributed to the defeated Confederate states, but I have never heard this explanation or many as complex or psychological from the people who typically spin ghost stories.)

It would be perfectly reasonable, of course, to suggest that the *spirit* of Lincoln can be felt at the historic site, which is part of a complex that includes the working theatre itself, a museum in its basement, and the house across the street where Lincoln died. And the current multimillion dollar renovations—which began in May 2007—are apparently being undertaken with an eye toward creating a "Lincoln Campus" centered on the theatre that will be a monument to the president's life and works, not just his death.

In the nearly nine-score years since it was built in 1833, Ford's Theatre has not always been known by that name nor has it always served as a place of entertainment. Its original function was as the First Baptist Church of Washington, and it served as such until 1861, when the congregation relocated to a new building and sold off the old one.

Career stage promoter John T. Ford purchased the former house of worship and converted it into a theatre that he dubbed Ford's Athenaeum, associating his own name with it for posterity. Fire gutted the building the following year, but Ford had it rebuilt and reopened it in 1863 as Ford's New Theatre.

Lincoln, who suffered from the immense stress of leading the United States through its greatest crisis before or since, enjoyed attending the theatre when he could as a distraction from his worries. Ford's New Theatre, located in the Northwest quarter of the city about eight blocks east of the White House and four blocks north of the National Mall, was a natural choice. It was thus that he and his wife were sitting in the theatre's "State Box" the evening of April 14, 1865, five days after rebel General Robert E. Lee surrendered his forces at Appomattox Court House, Virginia. Present with them were Army Major Henry Rathbone and his fiancée, Clara Harris. Absent were General Ulysses S. Grant and his wife, who had been invited by Lincoln but were otherwise occupied that night.

During the play, Booth stepped into the president's box, fired a .44-caliber derringer into the back of Lincoln's head, and stabbed Rathbone with a dagger. He then leapt onto the stage below and, before making good his escape, declared "Sic semper tyrannis!" (a Latin phrase that means "Thus always to tyrants," which seems an especially inappropriate label for a man who had freed an entire race from bondage). An unconscious Lincoln was taken across the street to a boarding house, the Petersen House. There, after being treated by physicians and visited by government officials throughout the night, he died the next morning at 7:22 A.M. He was 56.

The investigation that followed the assassination of Lincoln and the manhunt for Booth degenerated into a vicious witch hunt that resulted in many innocent people being imprisoned for various periods (and, perhaps, a few of them being put to death). Ford and his two brothers were among those rounded up and languished in prison thirty-nine days before being exonerated.

A year later, Congress authorized purchase of the theatre by the Federal government, which then forcibly seized the theatre and forever banned it from being used as a place of entertainment. It paid Ford $100,000 for his property despite his desire to keep it, further contributing to the bitterness he felt toward the government.

Ford's former theatre was soon after taken over by the U.S. military, which used it as the repository for War Department records, the library of the Surgeon General's Office, and the Army Medical Museum for a bit more than two decades. In 1887, the medical functions were removed from the building and it was thereafter used as a clerk's office for the War Department. Just six years later, however, the front section of the building collapsed, killing twenty-two of the clerks working there and injuring another sixty-eight of them. After the building was repaired the government used it only as a warehouse until 1931.

Two years later, the structure was transferred to the National Park Service, but sat unused for more than two decades. Then, in 1954, Congress approved funds for a restoration that began ten years later and was completed in 1968. Ford's Theatre was reopened for performances at that time and the Ford's Theatre Society, a nonprofit association, now has an exclusive contract with the National Park Service to stage plays at the site.

In 1970, both the theatre and the Petersen House—a brick, Federal-style rowhouse—were combined into the Ford's Theatre National Historic Site, which is currently administered by the

National Park Service. The museum beneath the theatre contains a large collection of "Lincolniana," including the original door to the theatre box where the shooting occurred, the president's coat, a variety of portraits and statues of Lincoln, the pistol used by Booth, and the assassin's diary.

Whether a ghost is among the things that can be associated with the site is, of course, an open question. If Ford's Theatre is really haunted, it is far more likely that the spirit of its namesake lingers at the place than it is that Lincoln's does. After all, the shabby way by which Ford was dispossessed of his property is certainly the classic sort of incident often associated with sites haunted by disgruntled spirits. Frankly, constantly being mistaken for either the slain president or his killer and having his own grievance perpetually ignored by those hoping or expecting to see someone else, would hardly mollify the unhappy spirit of Ford if it indeed haunts the building that bears his name.

Ghosthunting
Travel Guide

Visiting Haunted Sites

Each of the haunted sites in this book is located in one of six different geographical areas: the Northern, Central, Coast, Mountain, and Valley regions of Virginia, and Washington, D.C. A great many haunted sites in these various regions have some connection to the Colonial era or to the Civil War, two defining elements in the history of both the Commonwealth of Virginia and the District of Columbia.

All of the information in the following section has been verified to the best of my abilities — and was often what I used while working on this book — but ghosthunters are advised to confirm as much as possible before heading out into the field.

VIRGINIA

Virginia has an area of 42,774, square miles, making it the thirty-fifth largest state. It is bordered by Maryland and the District of Columbia to the north and east; the Atlantic Ocean to the east; North Carolina and Tennessee to the south; Kentucky to the west; and West Virginia to the north and west. The Commonwealth of Virginia is divided into thirty-nine independent cities and ninety-five counties.

Northern

Northern Virginia consists of Arlington, Fairfax, Loudoun, and Prince William counties, and the cities of Alexandria, Falls Church, Fairfax, Manassas, and Manassas Park. Important battlefields and other Civil War-themed attractions dot the region, most notably Manassas National Battlefield Park. Other attractions include Mount Vernon, home of George Washington, and the Pentagon.

⋇ **Arlington National Cemetery** (703) 607-8000
Arlington National Cemetery, Arlington, VA 22211
http://www.arlingtoncemetery.org

Spirits of those who have fallen over the past two centuries in the service of
their nation are believed to haunt many locations within this burial ground for
America's military personnel.

⋇ **Bunny Man Bridge**
Colchester Road (just south of the intersection with Fairfax Station Road)
Fairfax Station, VA 22039

While it is often described as being in Clifton, it is easier to find the correct section
of Colchester Road by treating it as a Fairfax Station location. This site is reputed
to be linked to a serial killer from the 1970s, whose spirit is said to make his
presence known in some way if his name is uttered three times. Bunny Man Bridge
may also have influenced scenes in at least one movie and one video game.

⋇ **Gadsby's Tavern** (703) 548-1288
138 North Royal Street, Alexandria, VA 22314
http://www.gadsbystavernrestaurant.com
gadsbys@verizon.net

A beautiful young woman who died at this historic tavern nearly two hundred
years ago is sometimes still seen there, as are a variety of other strange
phenomena.

⋇ **Manassas National Battlefield Park** (703) 361-1339
Park Visitor Center, 6511 Sudley Road, Manassas, VA 20109
http://www.nps.gov/mana

Site of the first major battle of the Civil War, ghosts of fallen soldiers have long
been seen roaming the fields where they fell during the bloodiest conflict in U.S.
history.
    HOURS: The park is open daily from dawn to dusk. The visitor's center is open
daily, 8:30 a.m.–5 p.m. It is closed on Thanksgiving and Christmas Day.

⋇ **Historic Occoquan** (703) 491-2168
Route 123 (a few miles west of I-95 south of Washington, D.C.)
Occoquan, VA 22125
http://www.occoquan.com

According to local legend, an Indian chief haunts a restaurant in this historic town; activity is said to be especially predominant upstairs in the ladies' restroom.

HOURS: Operating hours vary for the shops and restaurants, but most shops are closed daily by 5 p.m.

❧ Rippon Lodge (703) 792-6000
15520 Blackburn Road, Woodbridge, VA 22191

This Colonial-era home acquired a gruesome reputation for being haunted that it has only shaken in recent years. At this writing it was under renovation, so call for hours and visitation information.

❧ Weems-Botts Museum (703) 221-2218
Corner of Cameron and Duke Streets (Annex at 3944 Cameron Street)
Dumfries, VA 22026
http://historicdumfries.com/weemsbotts.html

Formerly the home of Mason Locke Weems, the man who fabricated the story of George Washington and the cherry tree, this site is now a museum and is said to be haunted by the ghosts of two women who dwelled there in the past century.

HOURS: The museum is open Tuesday–Saturday, 10 a.m.–4 p.m. No tours are given after 3:30 p.m.

Central

Much of the Civil War was fought within this broad region, which stretches from Spotsylvania County in the north to the North Carolina state line in the south, and links the coastal areas to the east with the valley and mountain regions to the west. Cities within it include Charlottesville, Danville, Fredericksburg, Lynchburg, Richmond, and Petersburg. Its counties include Appomattox, site of Robert E. Lee's surrender at the end of the Civil War, and Bedford, location of the National D-Day Museum. Attractions include Monticello, home of President Thomas Jefferson, and Montpelier, home of President James Madison.

⋇ Berry Hill Road
Berry Hill Road's northern end intersects with
Route 58 east of Danville.

Creepy under ideal conditions, this seven-and-a-half mile stretch of road
in Pittsylvania County and the ones leading off from it are home to ghosts,
abandoned farmsteads, blighted woodlands, rotting animal carcasses, an
uncanny number of vultures, gravitational anomalies, and "Satan's Bridge."

⋇ Exchange Hotel Civil War Hospital Museum (540) 832-2944
400 South Main Street, Gordonsville, VA 22942
http://www.hgiexchange.org

Once a historic hotel that served as a battlefield hospital during the Civil War,
this site is now a museum that is said to house the spirits of soldiers who died
from their wounds during the bloody conflict.
   HOURS: The Museum is open 10 a.m.–4 p.m., Monday, Tuesday, Thursday,
Friday, and Saturday. On Sundays, the Museum is open 1–4 p.m. Closed
Wednesdays and holidays. Museum is closed for the season: November 15–
April 1. Special tours, groups, and educational tours by appointment.

⋇ Poe Museum (804) 648-5523
1914–16 E. Main Street, Richmond, VA 23223
http://www.poemuseum.org

Located near to where Edgar Allan Poe lived and worked, this museum is
located in a historic house and contains a shrine to the troubled American
horror author. It is, perhaps almost naturally, believed by some to be haunted
by various ghosts.
   HOURS: The museum is open Tuesday through Saturday, 10 a.m.–5 p.m.,
Sunday, 11 a.m.–5 p.m., and is closed on Mondays.

⋇ The Trapezium House (804) 733-2400
244 N. Market Street, Petersburg, VA 23803

This early 19th century house contains no parallel walls, having been
constructed according to the guidance of a West Indian servant who advised
that building it in this way would ward off evil spirits. According to some, the
house is nonetheless haunted by the ghosts of former inhabitants.
   HOURS: This site is open to visitors only a few days a year and ghosthunters
are advised to call for more information before scheduling a visit.

✻ **Wreck of the Old 97 (Danville)** (434) 793-4636
Route 58/Riverside Drive (near the intersection with Highland Court)

Immortalized in the first recorded song to sell a million copies in the United
States, the Southern Express train "Old 97" plummeted into a ravine in 1903,
killing eleven people and injuring all but one of the others on board.

Coast

This section includes sites located in the Chesapeake Bay,
Eastern Shore, and Tidewater/Hampton Roads regions of Virginia. Its cities include Chincoteague Island, Norfolk, and Virginia Beach, home of psychic Edgar Cayce. Counties include
Accomack, Hampton, and Smithfield. It is the location of the
original settlements in the state and includes the historic triangle of Jamestown, Williamsburg, and Yorktown.

✻ **Assateague Lighthouse** (757) 336-3696
Assateague Island, VA
http://www.assateagueisland.com/lighthouse/lighthouse_info.htm

Built in 1867 to warn mariners of treacherous shoals around islands made
famous for their wild ponies, this site is believed by some to be inhabited in
death by those responsible for tending its light in life.
 HOURS: Assateague Lighthouse is open every Friday–Sunday, 9 a.m.–3 p.m.,
Easter weekend through Thanksgiving weekend

✻ **1848 Island Manor House** (757) 336-5436
4160 Main Street, Chincoteague Island, VA 23336
http://www.islandmanor.com

Built by two affluent professionals in 1848 as an impressive manor house, this
home played an important role during the Civil War and is today the most
historic B&B on Chincoteague. No fewer than three ghosts are believed to
haunt its chambers.

✻ **Colonial Williamsburg** (757) 229-1000
P.O. Box 1776, Williamsburg, VA 23187-1776
http://www.history.org

One of the oldest municipalities in the United States, the colonial-era heart of
Williamsburg is the site of numerous 18th-century buildings said to be haunted
by ghosts.

⁂ **Fort Monroe** (757) 788-3391
Casemate Museum, P.O. Box 51341, Hampton, VA 23651
http://www.monroe.army.mil (click on "Contact Us" and scroll down
to the link for "Casemate Museum").

In continuous usage by U.S. military forces for more than 170 years, this coastal
redoubt is the site of several famous hauntings and was the inspiration for
the Edgar Allan Poe story "The Cask of Amontillado." Public access to military
installations can vary, so please call the above number.

Mountain

Located in the far southwestern corner of the state, this
is Virginia's most isolated, sparsely populated, and beautiful
region and encompasses the Blueridge Highlands and Heart of
Appalachia sections of the state. Its cities include Bristol, Abingdon, and Blacksburg. Attractions include the Crooked Road,
"Virginia's Music Heritage Trail," and Mount Rogers, highest
point in the Commonwealth.

⁂ **Barter Theatre** (276) 628-2281
127 West Main Street, Abingdon, VA 24212
http://www.bartertheatre.com

Opened during the Great Depression, people in this isolated town could trade
homegrown produce for tickets to live entertainment that they otherwise would
not have been able to afford. It is believed by some to be home to numerous
ghosts, including that of its founder and some of the entertainers who once
worked upon its stage.

HOURS: The box office is open Monday and Tuesday, 10 a.m.–4 p.m.,
Wednesday–Saturday, 9 a.m.–5 p.m., Sunday, 1–5 p.m., and offers extended
hours for evening performances.

⁂ **Carroll County Courthouse** (276) 728-5397
515 North Main Street, Hillsville, VA 24343
http://www.VisitVirginiaBlueRidgeMountains.com

Tourism@VisitVirginiaBlueRidgeMountains.com

In 1912, a murderous spree at the conclusion of a trial claimed the lives of five people, including the sheriff and presiding judge. The site of those attacks, the Carroll County Courthouse, is believed by some to be haunted by the spirits of the slain, forever searching for justice.

HOURS: Monday, Tuesday, Thursday, and Friday (closed Wednesday, Saturday, and Sunday), 8:30 a.m.–4:30 p.m.

⁎ Devil's Den (276) 730-3100
80 Cemetery Road, Fancy Gap, VA 24328
http://www.hillsville.com/recreation_pgs/nature_trails_pgs/
devil_den.htm
CarrollTourism@ChillsNet.org

This cold, damp cave in the Blue Ridge Mountains has a history as a hiding place that goes back at least as far as the days of the Underground Railroad and was used as a refuge by some of the gunmen in the 1912 shooting at the nearby Carroll County Courthouse. It is also the site of multiple unquiet spirits.

HOURS: May–November, 8 a.m.–8 p.m.

⁎ Historic Sidna Allen Home (276) 728-2594
5935 Fancy Gap Highway (Route 52), Fancy Gap, VA 24328
http://www.VisitVirginiaBlueRidgeMountains.com/attractions.shtml
Tourism@VisitVirginiaBlueRidgeMountains.com

This beautiful Victorian home was owned by one of the shooters in the Carroll County Courthouse shooting and is believed by some to be haunted by his embittered spirit and possibly those of his family members.

⁎ Octagon House
631 Octagon House Road, Marion, VA 24354

This crumbling brick edifice is believed by many who have visited it to be haunted by the spirits of slaves who were tortured by the master of the house. It is abandoned and on private property, and ghosthunters are advised to exercise caution when visiting it.

⁎ U.S. Route 58

While it may not be actually haunted itself, the western stretch of Route 58 — a mountainous road that runs along Virginia's southern boundary running through Lee, Scott, Washington, Grayson, Carroll, and Patrick Counties —

passes by numerous ghost hamlets and is a useful thoroughfare for those hunting for haunted sites in this most isolated part of the Old Dominion. It runs from the far southwestern end of the state in the west to Virginia Beach in the east.

Valley

Virginia's Shenandoah Valley region, a portion of the Great Appalachian Valley, is bounded by the Blue Ridge Mountains to the east and the Appalachian and Allegheny Plateaus to the west and is named for the river which stretches much of its length. It encompasses several Virginia counties, including Augusta Clarke, Frederick, Page, Rockbridge, Rockingham, Shenandoah, and Warren. Cities within this region, from the south, include Roanoke, Staunton, Harrisonburg, Winchester, Lexington, Waynesboro, Front Royal, and Harpers Ferry, where the Shenandoah flows into the Potomac River.

❧ **Belle Grove Plantation** (540) 869-2028
336 Belle Grove Road, Middletown, VA 22645
http://www.bellegrove.org

This historic grain and livestock farm was once the centerpiece of a great 7,500-acre estate. Today, it is both a popular tourist attraction and the apparent home of several ghostly entities.

HOURS: Guided tours are offered daily April through October, and on select weekend days in November, including the Friday after Thanksgiving Day. Tours begin 15 minutes after each hour, departing from 10:15 a.m. until 3:15 p.m. Mondays through Saturdays, and from 1:15 to 4:15 p.m. on Sundays.

❧ **The Carriage Inn** (304) 728-8003
417 E. Washington Street, Charles Town, WV 25414
http://www.carriageinn.com
StayAtTheCarriageInn@comcast.net

Located just across the Virginia state line in Charles Town, West Virginia, this beautifully restored, Civil War-era bed-and-breakfast was both the location of a historic meeting during the war and the home of a Southern spy. It is also an ideal location for anyone exploring the area around the northern end of the Shenandoah Valley, and is convenient to historic areas like Harper's Ferry.

> **Cedar Creek Battlefield** (540) 868-9176
> 7718-1/2 Main Street, Middletown, VA 22645
> http://www.nps.gov/cebe

This battlefield has been the site of numerous apparitions in the years since one of the Civil War's bloodiest battles was fought on it.

HOURS: April 1–October 31, Monday–Saturday, 10 a.m.–4 p.m.; Sunday, 1–4 p.m. November 1–March 31, call (540) 869-2064 for an appointment.

> **Cork Street Tavern** (540) 667-3777
> 8 West Cork Street, Winchester, VA 22601

This restaurant is located in a building reputed to be haunted by at least two ghosts, one of which has a reputation for tripping female guests and staff.

> **Fuller House Inn** (877)-722-3976
> 220 W. Boscawen Street, Winchester, VA 22601
> http://www.fullerhouseinn.com

Located in a historic home with sections that date to the 18th century, this inn has been the site of numerous paranormal phenomena. It is also a great place to stay while exploring haunted places in and around Winchester and the northern end of the Shenandoah Valley.

> **Poor House Road Tunnel**
> Lexington, VA 24450

Local legends have long branded this out-of-the-way tunnel as the site of horrible events in the past. Various ghosthunting expeditions have collected evidence that it might, indeed, be haunted by troubled spirits of some sort. It is located about a half mile north of the intersection of Poor House Road and the old Valley Pike.

> **Village Square** (540) 667-8961
> 103 North Loudon Street, Winchester, VA 22601
> http://www.villagesquarerestaurant.com
> info@villagesquarerestaurant.com

Located in a building that once served as an apothecary and speakeasy, this fine-dining restaurant is now apparently the abode of numerous ghosts.

❧ **Virginia Military Institute** (540) 464-7207
111 Smith Hall, Lexington, VA 24450
http://www.vmi.edu

Strange occurrences of various sorts have been reported over the years at this state military college, including a weeping statue, a mural with moving figures, and a ghastly phantasm known as "the Yellow Peril."

❧ **The Wayside Inn** (540) 869-1797
7783 Main Street, Middletown, VA 22645
http://www.alongthewayside.com
info@alongthewayside.com

For more than 210 years, this inn in the heart of Virginia has catered to the needs of travelers. Visitors and staff members alike have had numerous experiences with the ghosts that have remained behind in its storied rooms.

DISTRICT OF COLUMBIA

Located along the northern banks of the Potomac River, Washington, D.C., was established in 1790 as the capital of the United States and is one of the few major planned communities in the country. It is bordered by Maryland to the northwest, northeast, and southeast and Virginia to the southwest. Features include a number of older historic communities like Georgetown that are encompassed by the district, national museums like the Smithsonian Institution, and governmental edifices like the Capitol and the White House.

❧ **Ford's Theater** (202) 638-2941
511 10th Street, NW, Washington, DC 20004
http://www.fordstheatre.org

Ever since President Abraham Lincoln was assassinated here by actor John Wilkes Booth while attending a showing of *Our American Cousin*, this small, historic theater has been the site of strange sightings and occurrences.

HOURS: Ford's Theatre and the museum on the lower level are currently closed for renovations and will reopen in winter 2009.

٭ **Stephen Decatur House** (202) 842-0920
1610 H Street, NW, Washington, DC 20006
http://www.decaturhouse.org

Located near the White House on Lafayette Square, this two-hundred-year-old house was tainted by untimely death and is reputed to be one of the most haunted places in the capital city.

HOURS: For cell phone tour hours, brochures can be picked up at the house Monday–Saturday, 10 a.m.–5 p.m., and Sunday, noon–4 p.m. The tour can be accessed 24 hours a day. Exhibit gallery tours are conducted Monday–Saturday, 10 a.m.–5 p.m., and Sunday, noon–4 p.m. House tour hours are Friday and Saturday, 10 a.m.–5 p.m., and Sunday, noon–4 p.m.

Ghostly Resources

WEB SITES

Following are a number of Web sites that can help prospective ghosthunters plan their expeditions. This list is deliberately limited, both because additional sites can be found easily enough with a bit of online research, and because so much of what is available is suspect or of limited value.

Appalachian Ghost Walks

http://www.appalachianghostwalks.com
This site is run by an organization that gives ghost tours of sites in the Appalachian Mountain region of Virginia and Tennessee.

Balls Bluff Battlefield

http://www.trimarpress.com/BallsBluffReport.html
This site is dedicated to the paranormal history of Balls Bluff Battlefield, near Leesburg, Virginia.

Center for Paranormal Research and Investigation

http://www.virginiaghosts.com/haunted_travel.php
This site for a paranormal research group based in Richmond, Virginia, includes numerous leads on possibly haunted sites.

Ghosts of America

http://www.ghostsofamerica.com/2/Virginia_Indian_Valley_
   ghost_sightings.html
This directory of "Ghost sightings from all across the United States" is organized by state.

Haunted Places in Virginia

http://theshadowlands.net/places/virginia.htm
Part of a nationwide directory, this site includes brief descriptions of hauntings at numerous locations throughout the state. It is compiled from third party sources, however, and not verified by the Webmasters, and must thus be used with caution.

The Haunted Traveler

http://www.hauntedtraveler.com
This site includes leads on numerous possibly haunted places in Virginia,
Washington, D.C., and a number of other areas.

Meeting Steam Washington, D.C., Ghosthunting Page

http://hometown.aol.com/waniehol/DCplaces.html
This site includes numerous descriptions for haunted places in the District of
Columbia, along with useful information for visitors like addresses and phone
numbers.

Michael J. Varhola

http://www.varhola.com
This personal site of author Michael J. Varhola contains additional information
that might be of interest to readers of this book.

The Midnight Society

http://www.midnightsocietyrva.com/lore.html
This site is dedicated to "documenting Virginia folklore, telling ghost stories in
the dark, strolling through cemeteries, and poking around historical sites."

Official Tourism Site of Washington, D.C.

http://www.washington.org
While not oriented toward ghosthunters, this site run by the city of Washington,
D.C., is an excellent resource for people planning trips into the nation's capitol.

StrangeUSA

http://www.strangeusa.com
This site goes beyond ghosthunting and is a nationwide directory of "haunted
buildings, places, urban legends, cemeteries, weird places, cool places, ghost
towns, and anything else that is worth your time to visit."

Washington DC Metro Area Ghost Watchers

http://www.dchauntings.com
This site is a "source for paranormal investigation of ghosts, hauntings,
and entities in Washington, D.C., Northern Virginia, Southern and Western
Maryland, and beyond the Beltway."

FURTHER READING

This section lists all of the titles used during the research for this book, along with a number of others that are listed for their potential value to ghosthunters in general and those operating in the Old Dominion in particular.

Alan, Ian. *Virginia Ghosts: They Are Among Us* (Sweetwater Press, 2005).

Alexander, John. *Ghosts: Washington's Most Famous Ghost Stories* (The Washington Book Trading Company, 1988).

Allen, J. Sidna. *Memoirs of J. Sidna Allen: A True Narrative of What Really Happened at Hillsville, Virginia* (Reliable Printing Company, 1956).

Amrhein, John, Jr. *The Hidden Galleon: The True Story of a Lost Spanish Ship and the Legendary Wild Horses of Assateague Island* (New Maritima Press, 2007).

Barefoot, Daniel W. *Haunted Halls of Ivy: Ghosts of Southern Colleges and Universities* (John F. Blair, Publisher, 2004).

Behrend, Jackie Eileen. *The Hauntings of Williamsburg, Yorktown, and Jamestown* (John F. Blair, Publisher, 1998).

Gregory, G. Howard. *History of the Wreck of the Old 97* (G.H. Gregory, 1992).

Guttridge, Leonard F. *Our Country, Right or Wrong: The Life of Stephen Decatur, the U.S. Navy's Most Illustrious Commander* (Tom Doherty Associates LLC, 2006).

Hauck, Dennis William. *National Directory of Haunted Places* (Penguin Books, 1994).

Holzer, Hans. *The Ghosts That Walk in Washington* (Ballantine Books, 1971).

Kachuba, John. *Ghosthunters: On the Trail of Mediums, Dowsers, Spirit Seekers, and Other Investigators of America's Paranormal World* (New Page Books, 2007).

Kachuba, John. *Ghosthunting Illinois* (Emmis Books, 2005).

Kachuba, John. *Ghosthunting Ohio* (Emmis Books, 2004).

Kaczmarek, Dale. *Field Guide to Spirit Photography: The Essential Guide to Cameras in Paranormal Research* (Ghost Research Society Press, 2002).

Kaczmarek, Dale. *Illuminating the Darkness: The Mystery of Spook Lights* (Ghost Research Society Press, 2003).

Kaczmarek, Dale. *National Register of Haunted Locations* (Ghost Research Society).

Lee, Marguerite DuPont. *Virginia Ghosts* (Virginia Book Company, 1966).

Okonowicz, Ed and Kathleen. *Crying in the Kitchen: Stories of Ghosts That Roam the Water* (Myst & Lace Publishers Inc., 1998).

Rutherford, Mac. *Historic Haunts of Winchester: A Ghostly Trip Through Winchester's Past* (Lucky Books, 2003).

Sturgill, Mack. *Abijah Thomas and His Octagonal House* (M.H. Sturgill, 1990).

Taylor, L.B., Jr. *Civil War Ghosts of Virginia* (Progress Printing Co. Inc., 1996).

Taylor, L.B., Jr. *The Ghosts of Virginia* (Progress Printing Co. Inc., 1997).

Taylor, L.B., Jr. *The Ghosts of Tidewater* (Progress Printing Co. Inc., 1990).

Taylor, L.B., Jr. *The Ghosts of Williamsburg, Volume II* (Progress Printing Co. Inc., 1999).

Tennis, Joe. *Beach to Bluegrass: Places to Brake on Virginia's Longest Road* (Overmountain Press, 2007).

Tennis, Joe. *Southwest Virginia Crossroads: An Almanac of Place Names and Places to See* (Overmountain Press, 2004).

Acknowledgments

WRITING A BOOK IS MUCH LESS of a solo activity than people might think — as is ghosthunting under ideal conditions — and there are a number of people I would like to thank for efforts that range from routine to extraordinary.

Foremost among the people who deserve recognition is my wife, Diane, who accompanied me for much of the fieldwork and whose moral and logistical support made the completion of this book possible — and she deserves credit for guarding the car at a great number of the possibly haunted sites that I investigated. She also played a big part in compiling the information for the "Visiting Haunted Sites" section at the end of this book.

Just as important to this endeavor was my father, Michael H. Varhola, whose greatest contribution to this book was serving as primary author for two of its chapters, the ones on Fort Monroe in Hampton, Virginia, and the Stephen Decatur House in Washington, D.C. He also accompanied me on the excursion for one of the other chapters and provided useful guidance on a number of others.

Special thanks are due to the people who accompanied me on the field trips to the various sites described in this book. These include my mother Merrilea, my friends Geoff Weber and Jason Froehlich, my daughters Lindsey and Hayley, and my grandparents James and Valerie Beall.

Heartfelt thanks are also due to the people who extended their hospitality to us during the travel required for this book. These new friends include Jerry Prewitt of the 1848 Island Manor House on Chincoteague Island, Debby Johnson and Richie Oram of the Fuller House Inn in Winchester, and Ron and Deena McKinney of the Volunteer Gap Inn and Cabins in Fancy Gap.

I would also like to thank all the people — both those named in the various chapters of this book and those who for whatever reasons are unnamed — who took the time to speak with me about the sites described in this book and to show me around, such as Paul Carbé of Gadsby's Tavern; Beth Cardinale of the Weems-Botts Museum; Tina Carlson of The Shadowlands; Col. Keith Gibson and Cadet Dominique Baker of Virginia Military Institute; Roger Hawthorne of the Carroll County Chamber of Commerce; Dale Kaczmarek of the Ghost Research Society; Katherine Kiss of Guinevere's Antique Shop; Robert M.W. Kocovsky of the Exchange Hotel Civil War Hospital Museum; Judge Oliver A. Pollard Jr. of the Trapezium House; Courtney Prebich and Henry Ward of the Metropolitan Washington Airports Authority; Fairfax County Police Officer Kathryn Schroth; Chris Semtner of the Edgar Allan Poe Museum; David Smith of the Village Square Restaurant; Joel Smith of the Cork Street Tavern; Terri Vanderlaan of Virginia Paranormal; Colie Walker of Danville, Virginia; Laurel Wilkerson of the Chincoteague National Wildlife Refuge; and Peter Yonka of the Barter Theatre.

Two other people who deserve my thanks are authors Joe Tennis and John Amrhein Jr., whose books helped me while working on various parts of this project, and both of whom very generously provided me with useful information.

People beyond those mentioned above who are due thanks include Robert Harvey and a number of librarians of the Fairfax County Public Library system, especially those working in the Virginia Room at the City of Fairfax Regional Library.

Last but certainly not least are two people who have been of immeasurable help with this project, my editors Jack Heffron and John Kachuba, both of whom have provided me with invaluable guidance and feedback throughout its course.

Finally, I would like to beg the forgiveness of anyone I have neglected to mention here! Your help is no less appreciated because of this oversight.

ABOUT THE AUTHOR

Photo by Geoff Weber

MICHAEL J. VARHOLA is a freelance author, editor, and lecturer who specializes in nonfiction and travel-related subjects, and he runs Skirmisher Publishing LLC, a small game manufacturing company. He has a lifelong interest in the paranormal and has conducted investigations worldwide. He has been a resident of Fairfax County, Virginia, since 1991. His other books include *Everyday Life During the Civil War, Shipwrecks and Lost Treasures: Great Lakes,* and *Fire and Ice: The Korean War, 1950–1953.* He studied in Denver and Paris before earning a degree in journalism from the University of Maryland, College Park.